Flat Plane
Carving the Nativity

AF271660

Lynn Diel

Schiffer Publishing Ltd®

4880 Lower Valley Road, Atglen, PA 19310 USA

Dedication

This book is dedicated to my wife, Beverly, who has been a constant source of support and encouragement through good times and difficult times during our journey through life together. It is also dedicated to Bill Judt and Paul McCain for their wisdom, guidance, and encouragement. Above all, I thank God for His strength and guidance and for the abilities He has given me. *Sola Deo Gloria*.

Acknowledgments

Many thanks to David Berg, a great carver and a good friend, who took the time to get me started in carving. Thanks also to my students, who have been my best teachers.

Published by Schiffer Publishing Ltd.
4880 Lower Valley Road
Atglen, PA 19310
Phone: (610) 593-1777; Fax: (610) 593-2002
E-mail: Info@schifferbooks.com

For the largest selection of fine reference books on this and related subjects, please visit our web site at
www.schifferbooks.com
We are always looking for people to write books on new and related subjects. If you have an idea for a book please contact us at the above address.

This book may be purchased from the publisher.
Include $3.95 for shipping.
Please try your bookstore first.
You may write for a free catalog.

In Europe, Schiffer books are distributed by
Bushwood Books
6 Marksbury Ave.
Kew Gardens
Surrey TW9 4JF England
Phone: 44 (0) 20 8392-8585; Fax: 44 (0) 20 8392-9876
E-mail: info@bushwoodbooks.co.uk
Free postage in the U.K., Europe; air mail at cost.

Copyright © 2006 by Lynn Diel
Library of Congress Control Number: 2005934472

Designed by Joseph M. Riggio Jr.
Type set in Zapf Chancery Bd BT/Dutch 801 Rm BT

ISBN: 0-7643-2439-X
Printed in China

Contents

Patterns

Introduction

The beauty of these carvings lie in their simplicity, as well as the inherent symbolism of what they represent. The figures are "faceless" and without expression so as not to take away from the effect or from the intent of the carving.

— Comment by Rod Schrivener, Kearney, MO
Seminar student

The tradition of making and decorating a crèche (crib) at Christmas time is said to have originated in Greccio, Italy, in the early thirteenth century. History informs us that in 1223 St. Francis of Assisi created the first live, outdoor Nativity scene. St. Francis gathered a donkey, an ox, and several peasants to present a living reenactment of the first Nativity to celebrate Christmas.

The practice of celebrating the birth of Jesus had long been a subject that inspired painters and sculptors throughout the ages. Remembrances of Christ's birth that night in Bethlehem were made even in ancient times, as is evident in paintings found in the catacombs dating back to the third or fourth centuries. It is interesting to note that in many of the early paintings, four Magi were included rather than the three we see today. Also, Joseph was not present in many of the early Nativity scenes. It would take several centuries before he became a regular part of the scene.

Nativity scenes became very popular throughout Europe in the sixteenth century and began appearing in the private chapels of royal castles and aristocratic palaces. The Renaissance nobility considered nativity scenes the most prestigious gifts that they could give.

Over the years, I have worked with many carvers who wanted to carve Nativity sets for their children and grandchildren. Many of these carvers lost interest after completing their first set due to the amount of detail and the painting involved. Recognition of these difficulties led me to design the Nativity presented here in a method known as flat plane carving. Flat plane carving was popularized by the work of Emil Janel in the past and Harley Refsal and Ron Wells in the present. This carving style has gained popularity due to the simple flat planes and a minimalist approach to detail. The beauty of the carving is in the large flat planes that reflect light and provide lines to draw your eyes to the things that are important. This nativity set, then, is more easily carved since the emphasis in on the long flat planes and not on faces or other details. Finishing is made easier as well by the use of only a light Burnt Sienna stain. These simplifications allow the carver more time to make multiple sets to be shared with loved ones.

Just a note before we begin: As carvers, we have spent most of our time rounding the wood to obtain the look we want; however, in flat plane carving, the goal is to obtain large flat areas, so resist the urge to round. *Now*, let's get started!

Tools

You will only need a few tools to carve the nativity set in Flat Plane style.

V tool 60° - 3/8 inch (8mm)
#3 – 1/2 inch (12mm) or equivalent
#7 – 1/2 inch (12mm) or equivalent
#7 – 5/8 inch (16mm) or equivalent
3/16 inch, 6 inch long drill bit
Small battery powered drill
Knife – 2-1/4 inch thin blade or equivalent*
320-400 grit sandpaper (worn) for softening the edges

*I prefer Ron Well's carving knives because they are designed for flat plane carving. They have thin blades that allow carvers to make large flat planes as well as clean cuts across the grain and they hold a sharp edge with minimal maintenance. Ron's knives can be seen at the following web page: http://www.ronwellswoodcarving.com or he can be contacted at Ron Wells Woodcarving, HCR 32, Box 141, Mount Judea, AR 72655.

I wear a protective glove when I carve as defense against cuts that might be incurred while carving. It is not merely a question of the knife slipping, which it surely will from time to time, but when it does, where will it end up? Remember the cost of the glove is cheaper than a trip to the Emergency Room!

Finish

Winton™ Burnt Sienna Oil Paint
Mineral Spirits (Odorless)
Bartley™ Gel Varnish
Brush

Chapter One
Mary

The beauty of this design is that once you have mastered the steps for one of the nativity pieces, you are ready to carve the rest of the set. Each of the pieces varies a little from the other, i.e. height of the hands, head, etc. We will start with Mary, since this piece is the simplest and provides the foundation for all the rest of the pieces.

You will need a 2 inch by 2 inch by 5-1/4 inch block of Basswood to carve Mary. The first step is to establish the shoulder line as shown below.

1. Using a ruler, mark a line two inches from the top and continue this line around the block. Alternatively, you can use another 2 inch block as a reference as shown here.

2. The growth rings are indicated in the photo shown. Note how the rings end at a corner (A/B). It is recommended to select either of these ends for the front. Select one corner and place a small "F" on that corner to indicate the front.

3. To obtain the large flat planes for the carving, we will begin by drawing lines that will serve as guidelines for our cuts. Start by drawing a line from one corner to the other corner on the top of the block. Now draw a line from the back corner and stop at the middle. Note that we do not draw a line to the Front as shown by (F).

The next step is to select which of the corners we will use as the front of the carving. I typically will look at the growth rings and try to select a block where the growth rings end at a corner. By selecting one of these corners, it allows for the details that will be carved to have the most structural strength. If the growth rings are perpendicular to the sides, then any corner will work.

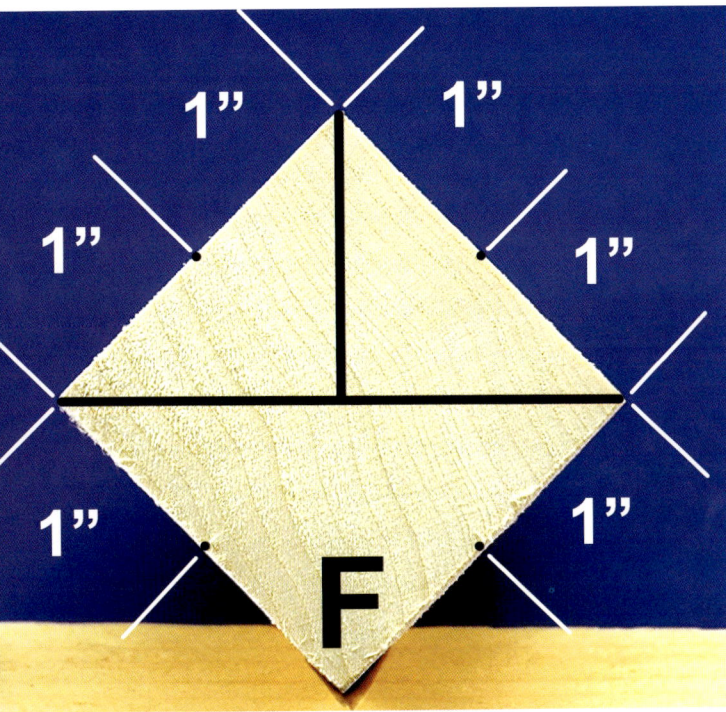

4. Mark off the midpoints for each of the sides. For the 2 inch block these will be at 1 inch from each corner.

5. Draw lines from the center of each midpoint on the sides.

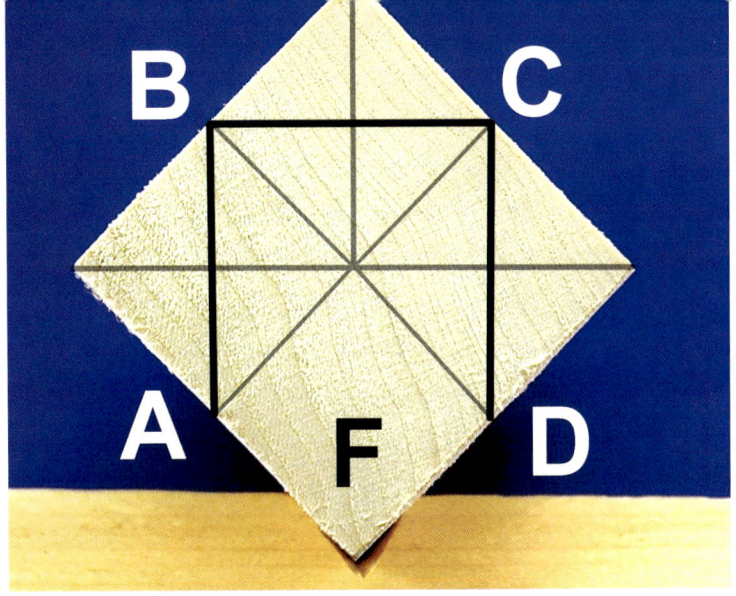

6. Connect the ends of the lines (A) to (B) to (C) and then to (D). These lines will provide the guidelines for the sides of the shoulder and head area.

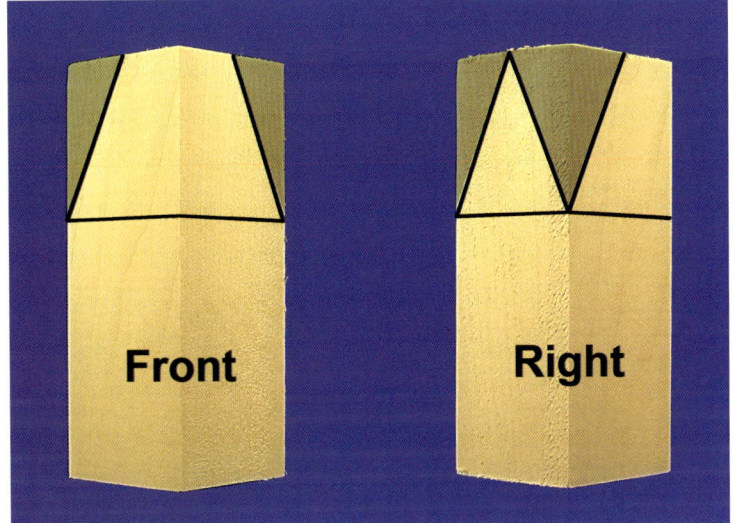

7. Turn the block so that the front is facing you. Connect the lines from the top (middle) to the corners at the shoulder line. Continue this around to the right side.

8. Continue to rotate the block so that the back is facing you. Connect the lines from the top (middle) to the corners at the shoulder line. Continue this to the left side. This will mark off the corners of the block that you will be removing in the following steps.

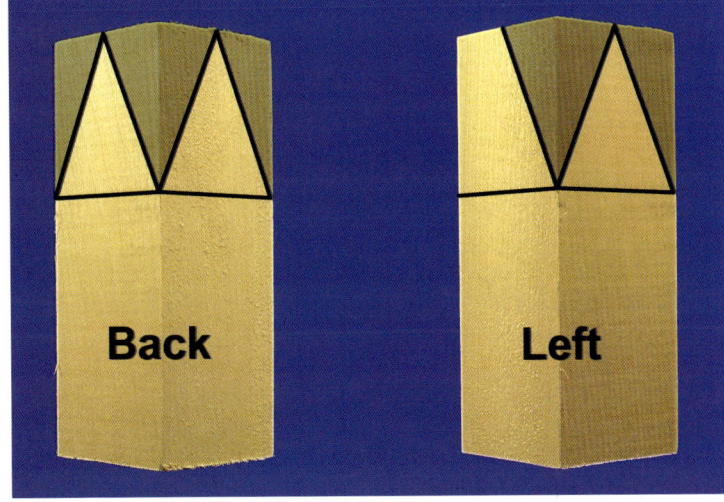

9. Using a knife, remove the wedge (shaded area) on the corner. Try to make long flat cuts to obtain the Flat Plane look.

11. The block should be taking on this shape from the front. In later steps we will be marking and removing the wood for the face and hands.

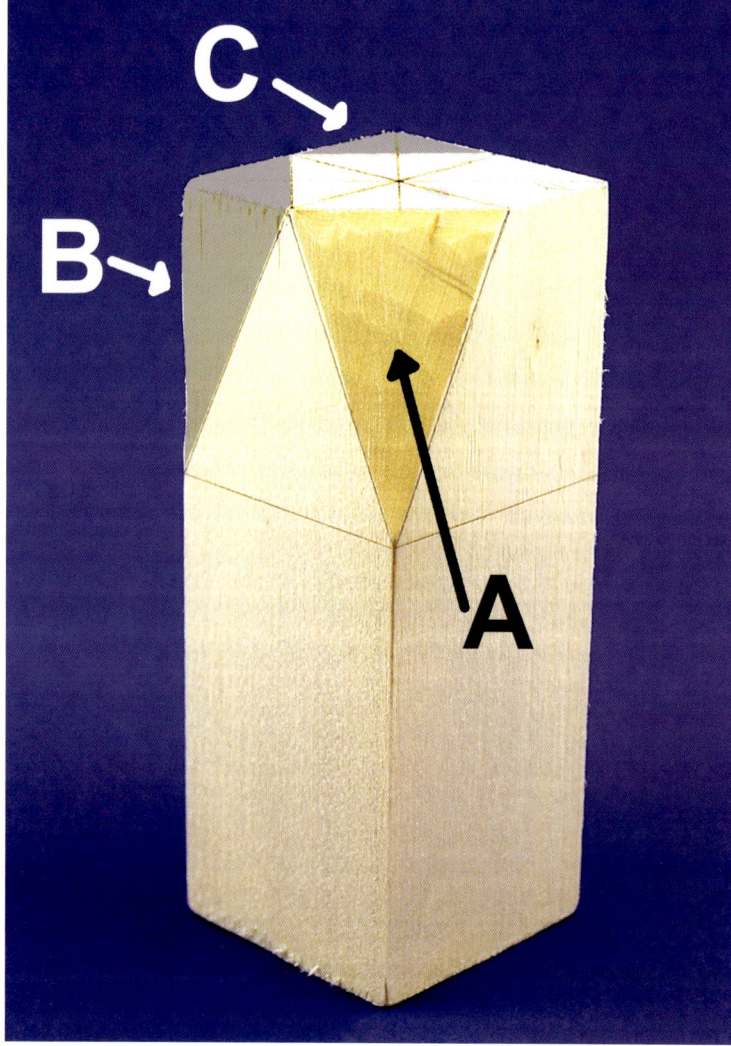

10. Progress so far. Note the large flat plane as indicated by (A). Continue removing the wedges on the other two sides as indicated by (B) and (C).

12. Note how the three sides are tapering towards the top. This is the first step towards blocking out the carving. We will need to make additional cuts to bring the head and shoulders forward to allow for the appearance that Mary is kneeling and her head is bent down slightly.

13. Progress so far. The top of the block should look like the photo shown. Note that the Front, as indicated by (F), is not removed at this time.

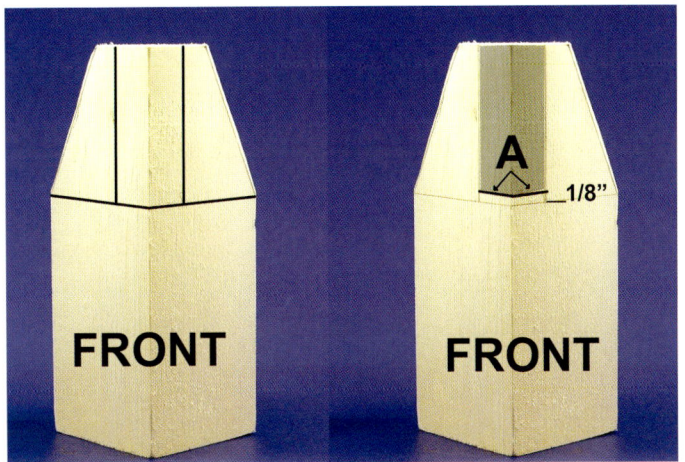

15. Progress so far is shown on the left. Mark a line 1/8 inch above the shoulder line as shown by (A) in the photo on the right. The shaded area is what will be removed in later steps. This measurement (above or below the shoulder line) will change as you carve the various figures. Since Mary is traditionally smaller in size, the top of the robe covering her hands will appear above the shoulder line. When carving Joseph and the Shepherd, the top of the robes will fall below the shoulder line.

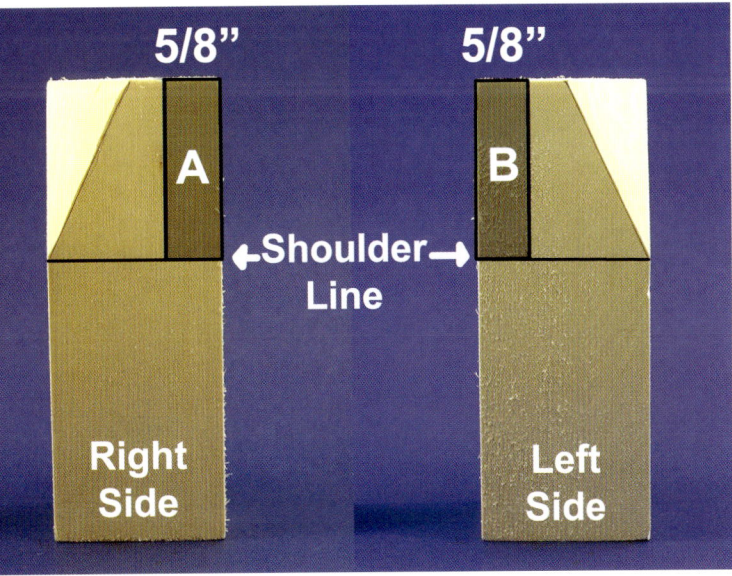

14. Measure 5/8 inch from the front edge and place a mark. Draw a line from this mark down to the shoulder line as indicated by (A). Repeat this step for the other side as shown in (B).

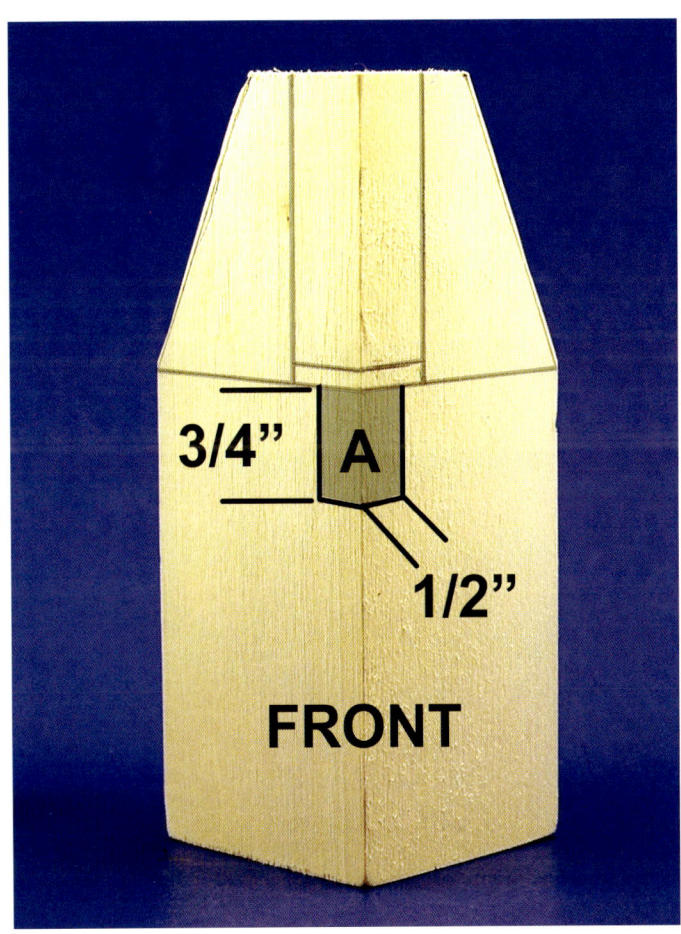

16. Measure 1/2 inch from the front edge to both sides and make a mark with the pencil. Now, measure down 3/4 inch from the shoulder line for the base of the hands as shown and draw a line from the edge to the 1/2 inch line as shown in (A). This defines the width and length of the hands.

17. The inside and the outside of the robe have a gentle curve flowing from the top of the hands to the base. You can draw these lines in free hand or use the templates that are supplied.

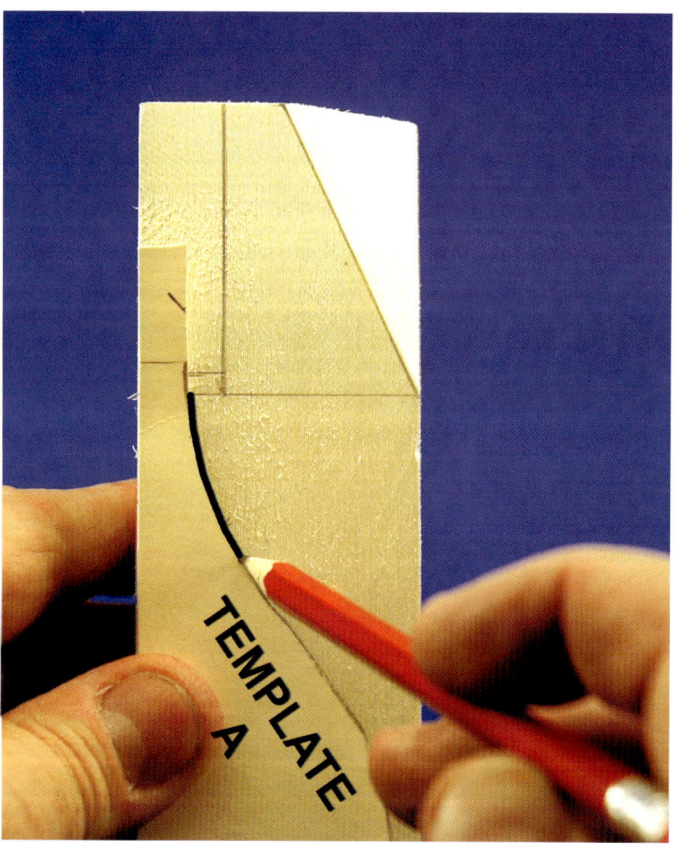

18. Using Template A, draw in the lines that will form the inside of the hands and the robe. Do this for both sides.

19. Draw in the line that will form the outside of the robe either by free hand or using Template B. Do this for both sides.

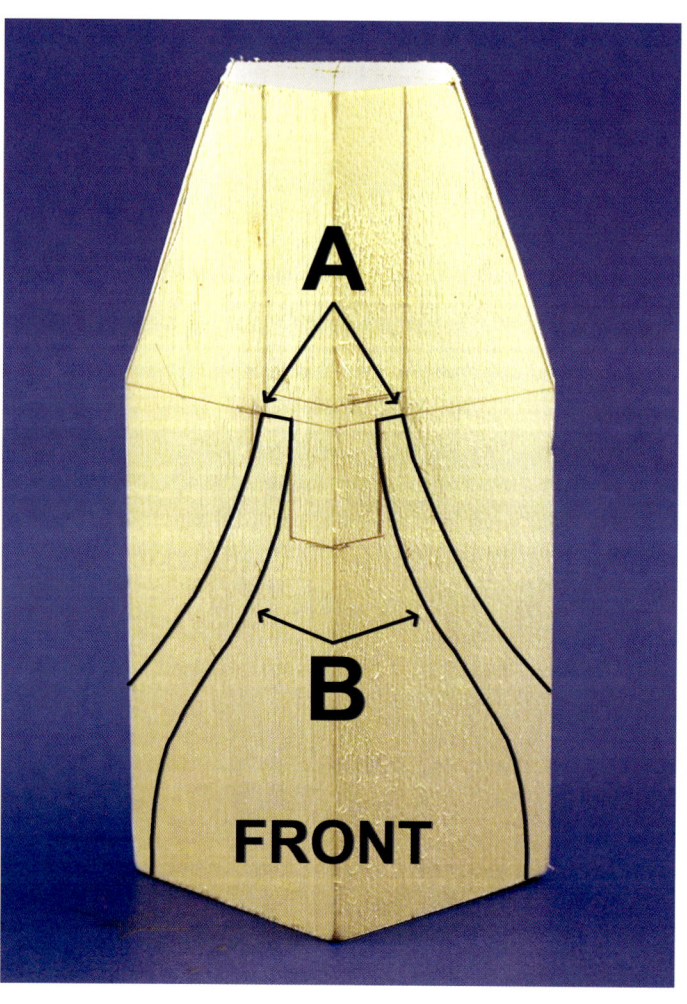

20. Progress so far. The block should look like this from the front.

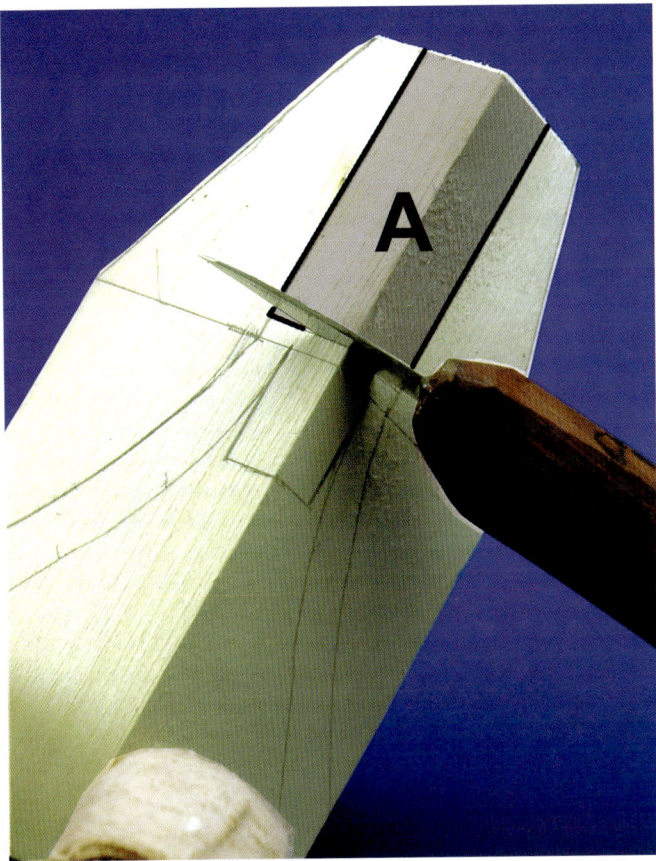

21. Make a stop cut at the top of the robe as shown. You will be removing the shaded area that is labeled (A).

22. We will start by removing a small wedge above the robe. Make a cut with the knife to remove the wood. Repeat steps 21 and 22 until you have reached the depth as shown.

23. Remove the rest of the wood between the two lines that defines the width of the face area.

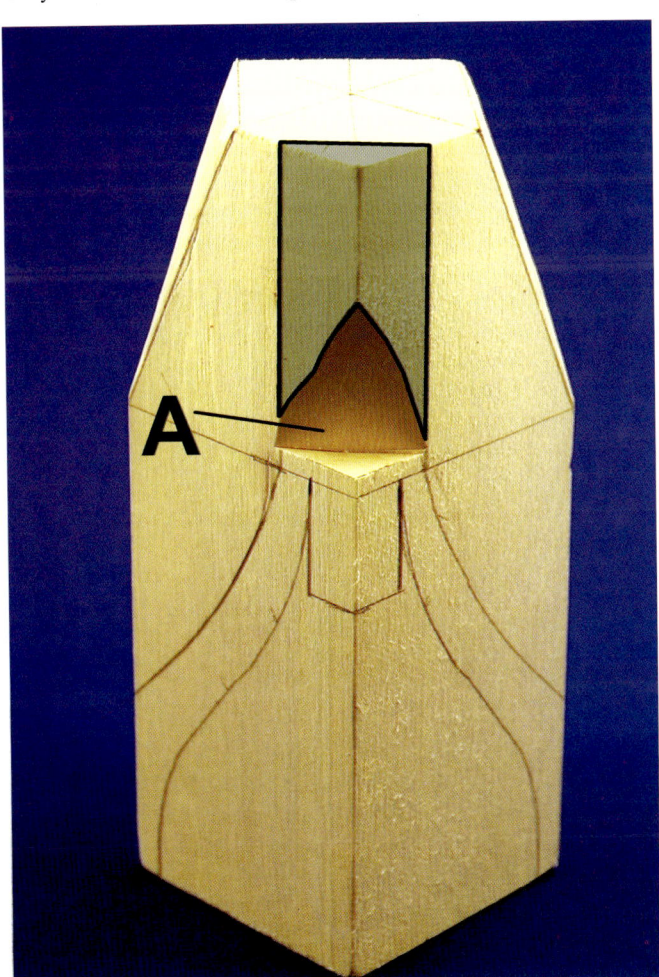

24. The top of the block should look like the photo shown.

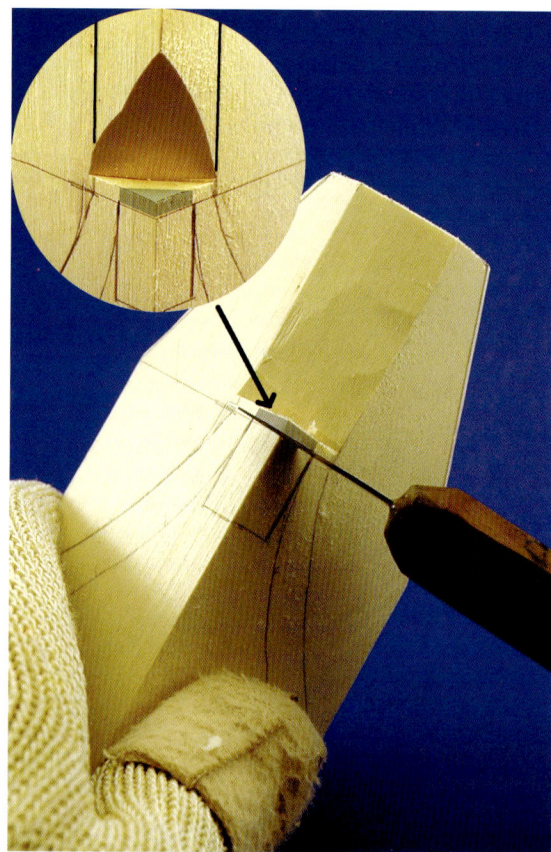

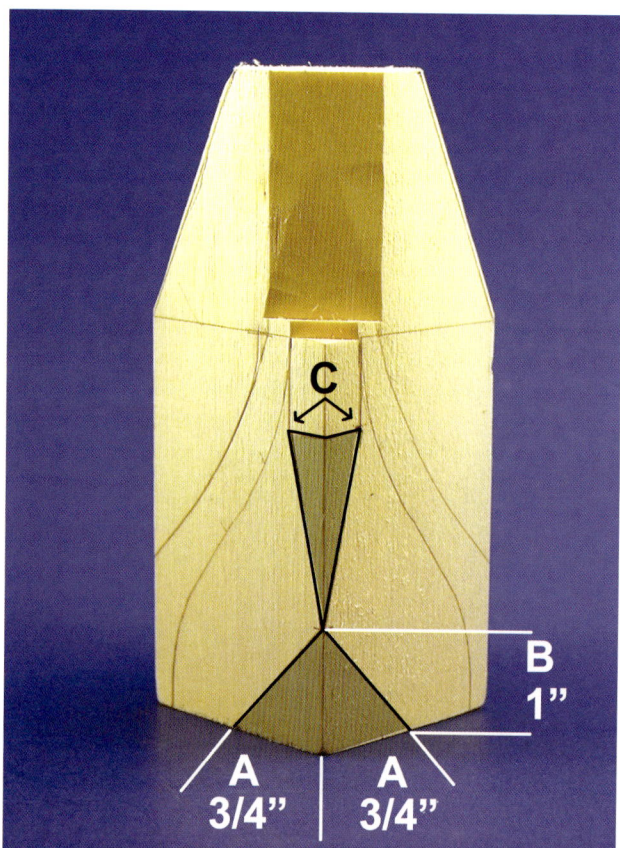

25. Next we mark off the area where the robe is behind the hands as shown in the shaded area (inset). Using the knife, make a stop cut and gently remove the wood.

27. Measure 3/4 inch from the edge of the block at the base as shown by (A). Measure 1 inch from the bottom along the front edge. Draw a line from this point to the two points that you located 3/4 inch from the edge. Draw a line from the top of this triangle to the base of each side of the hands. These lines represent the wood that will be removed in later steps and will provide the appearance that Mary is kneeling.

26. Progress so far. This cut will allow for a small step above the hands, which will represent the robe going over Mary's hands. The top of the hands and the robe should look like (A).

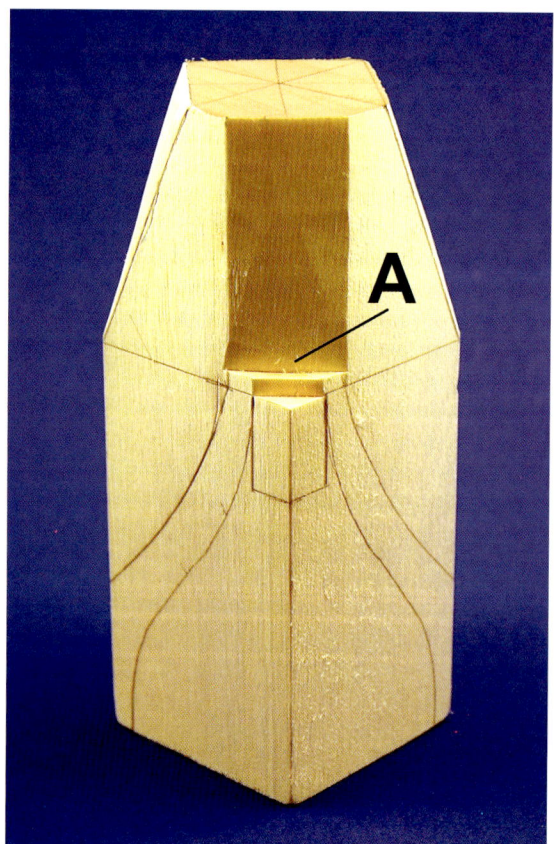

28. Take the knife and remove the wedge (shaded area) at the bottom.

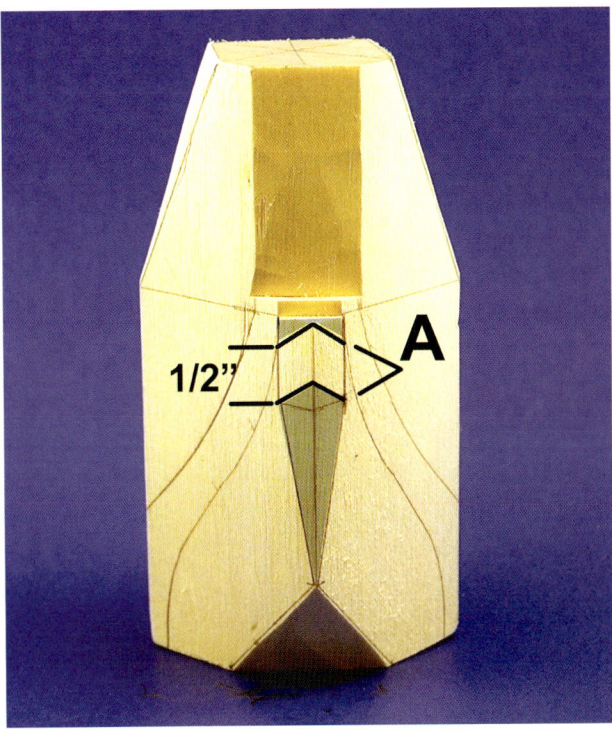

29. The hands will be represented as praying for Mary. Locate and mark the block 3/8 inch down on both sides of the hands. Draw a line from these marks to the peak (front edge) of the hands. Locate and mark the block 1/2 inch from this point down the front of the block. Draw a line from this point to the base on each side of the hands.

31. Next we will remove the wood shown shaded. You may need to make several passes to obtain the depth.

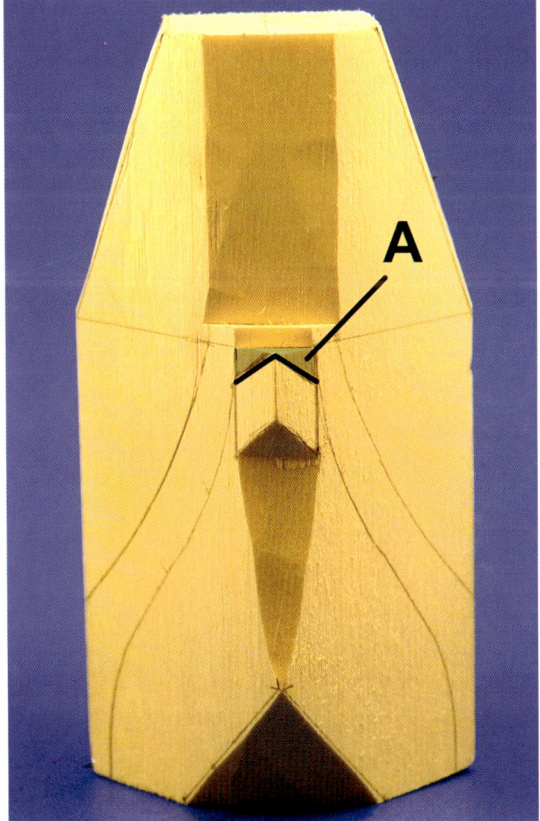

30. Make a stop cut across the base of the hands as shown in the photo and remove the wood as shown. You may need to make several passes to obtain the depth.

32. The tops of the hands form an A-frame shape. Make a stop cut straight into the front of the hands as shown by (A). Take your time and make small, careful cuts.

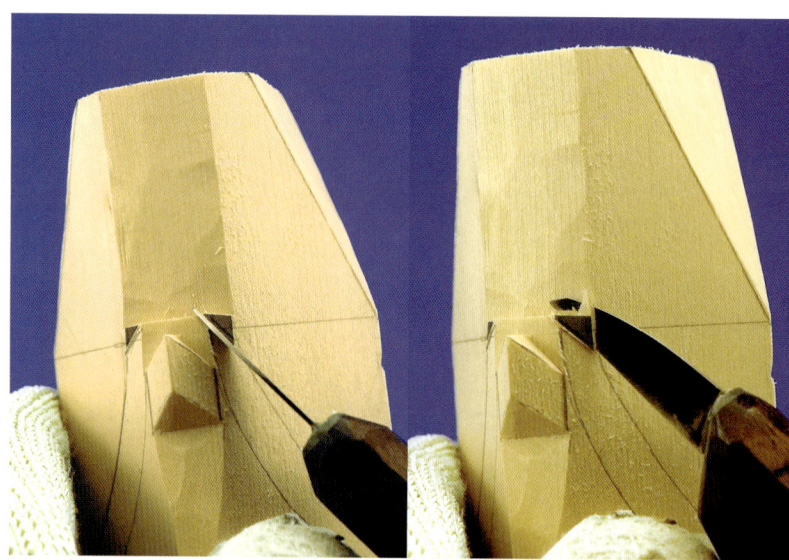

35. Make a stop cut straight into the front of the block as shown in the left photo. Now slide the knife down the back side and remove the wedge (right).

33. Make a stop cut along side the back of the hands as shown. Take your time and make careful cuts. The wedge should drop off.

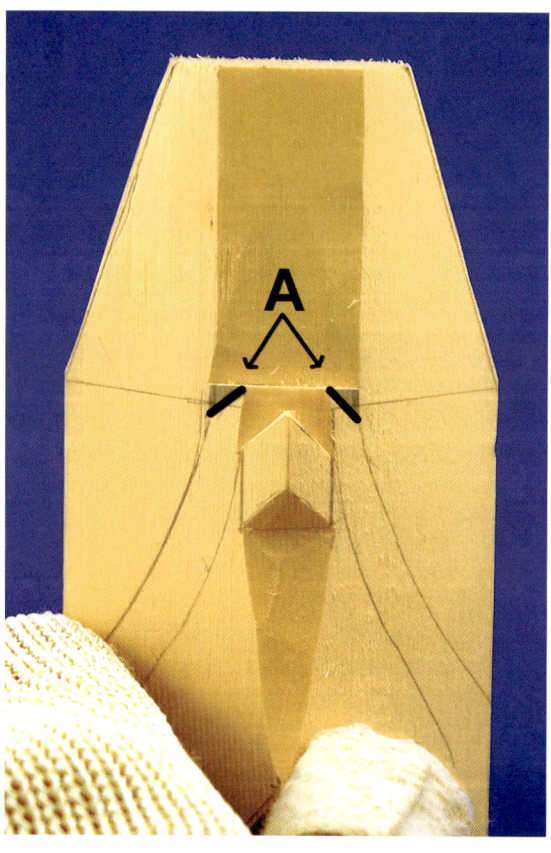

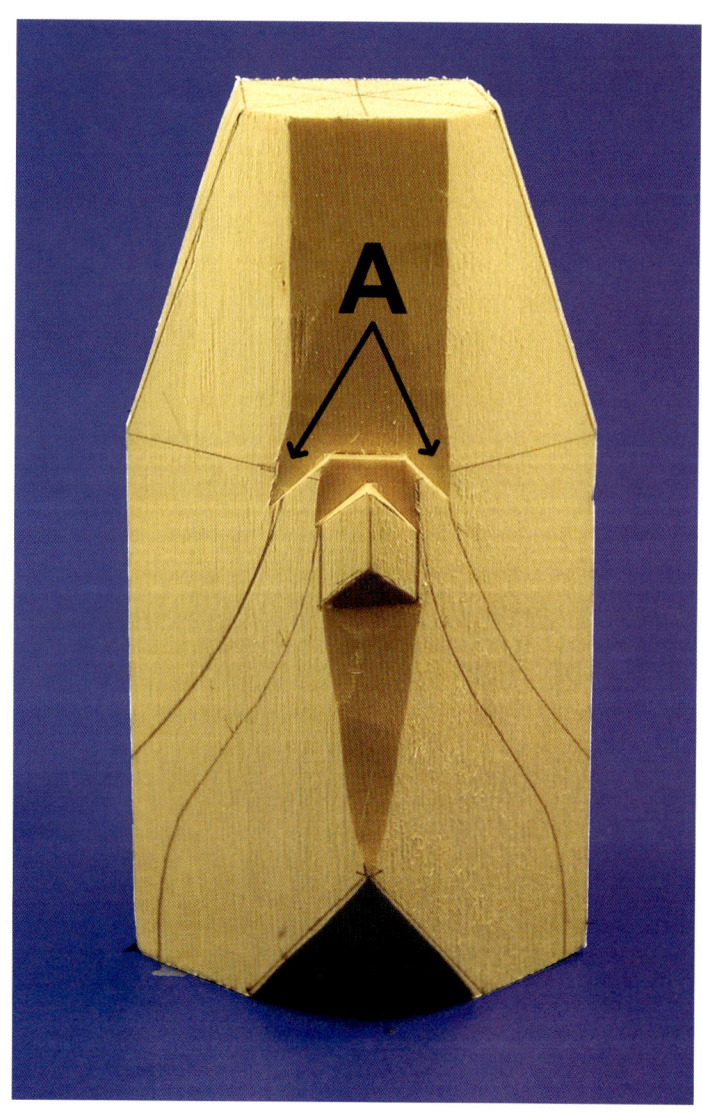

34. Next we will remove the wood that is on top of the robe that drapes over the hands. Mark a line at a 45 degree angle on the outside of the robe as shown in (A).

36. Progress so far. Next, we will extend the robe down alongside the body. We will start these cuts at the points indicated by (A).

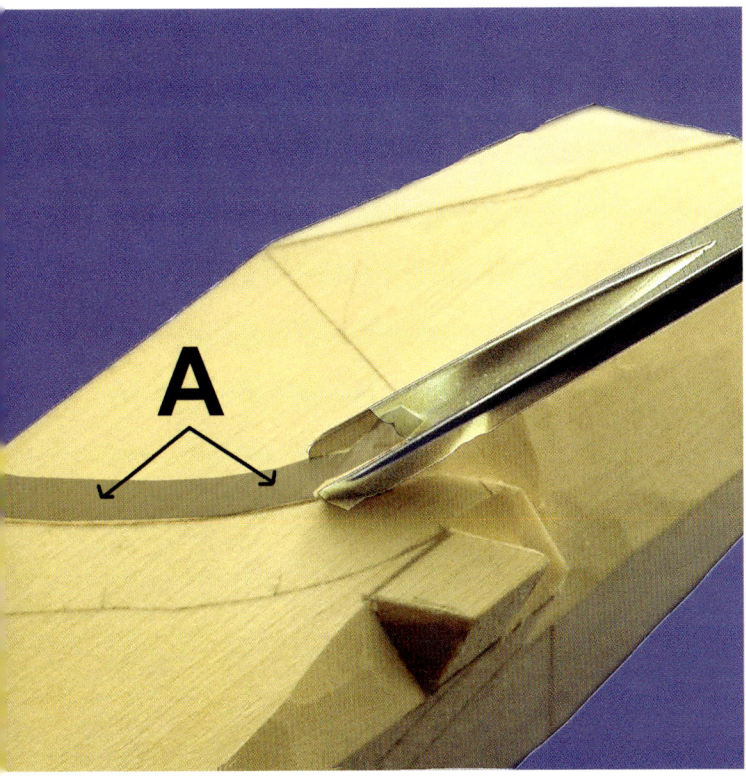

37. Take the V-tool and remove the wood that is shaded. Tilt the V-tool so that the straight edge of the tool is vertical to the top of the robe as shown in the photo.

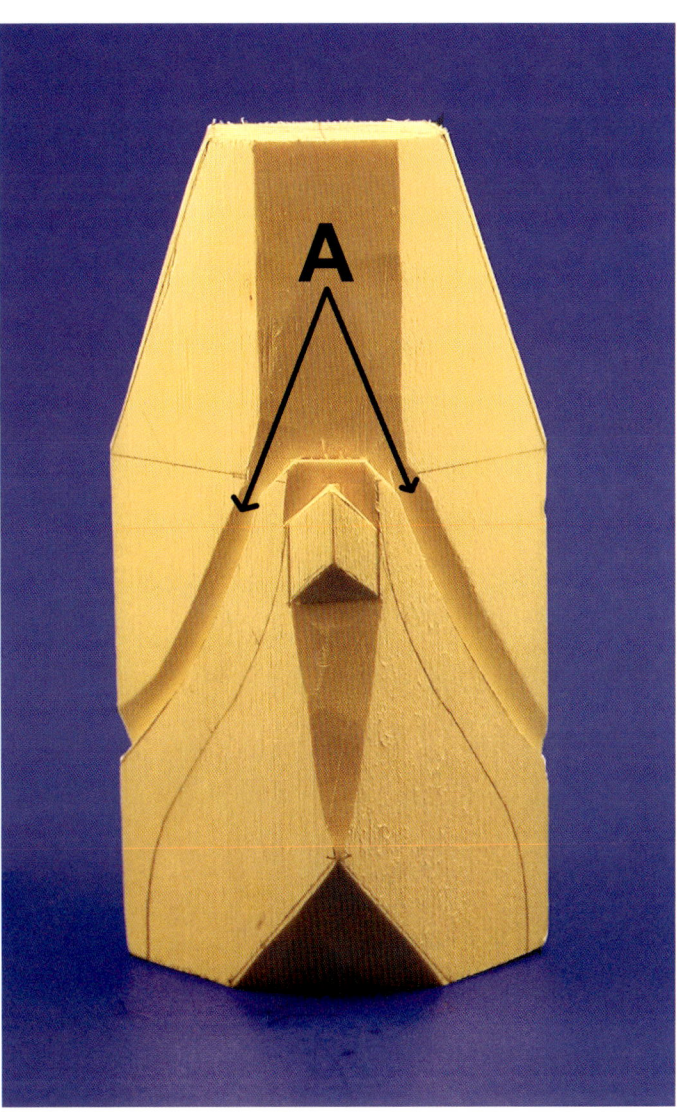

39. Progress so far. Don't be concerned if the two sides are not exactly alike. There can be some subtle differences and it will look fine.

38. Take the V-tool and make the same cut on the other side. Remember to tilt the V-tool so that the straight edge of the tool is vertical to the block.

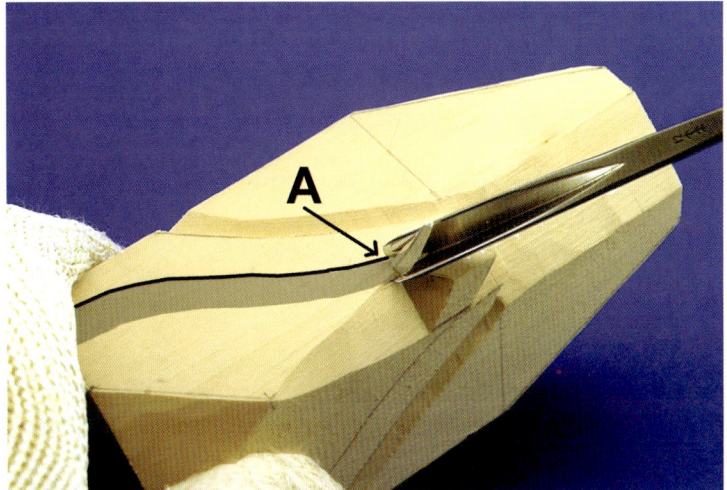

40. Next we will remove the wood below the robe where it meets the tunic. Take the V-tool and remove the wood that is shaded. Tilt the V-tool so that one edge is vertical with the bottom of the robe.

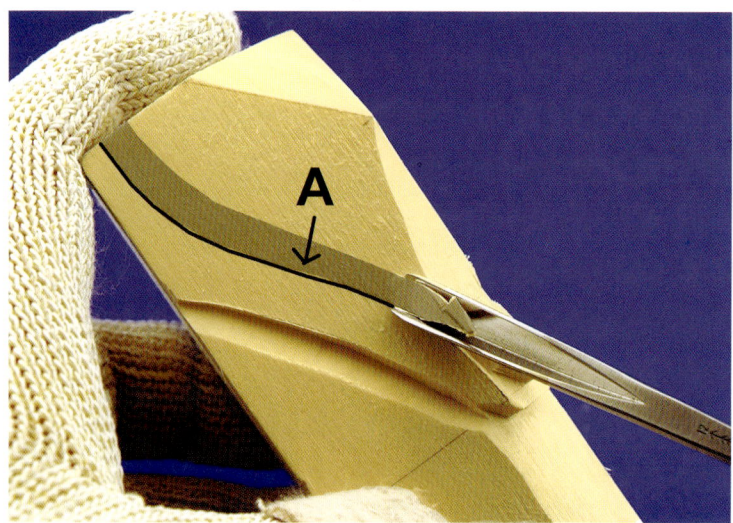

41. To make the next cut on the other side; it helps to turn the block over to make the cut.

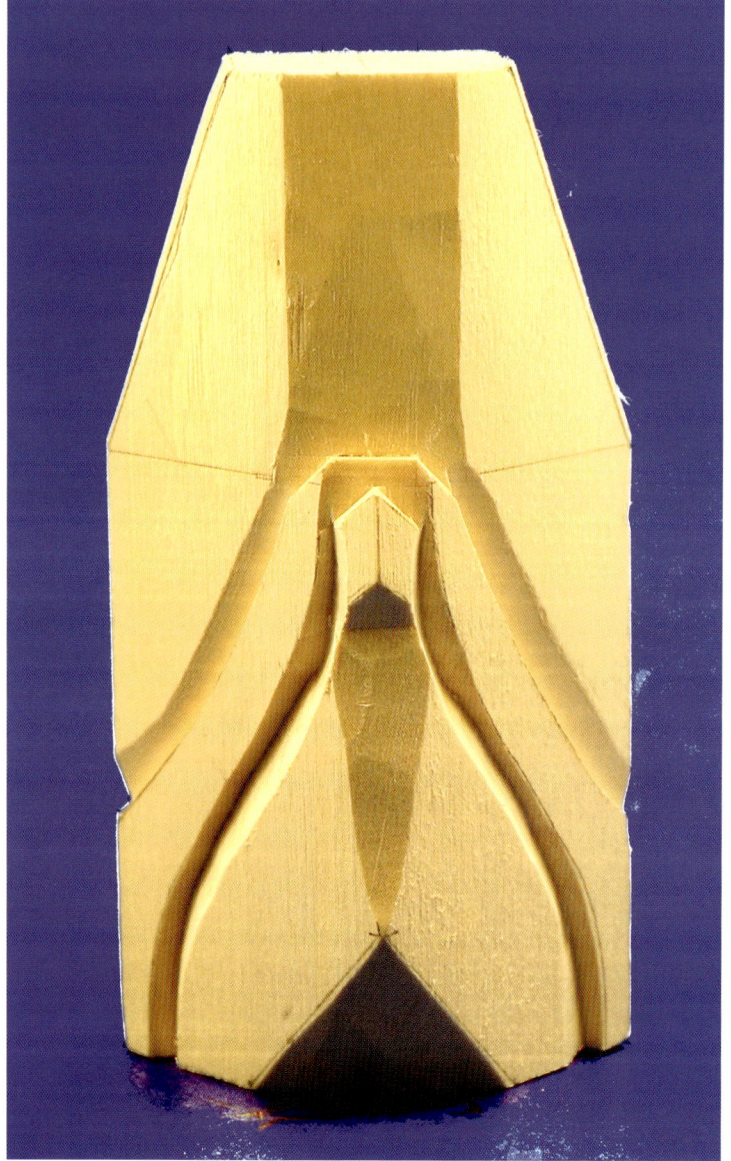

42. Progress so far. The carving is beginning to take shape.

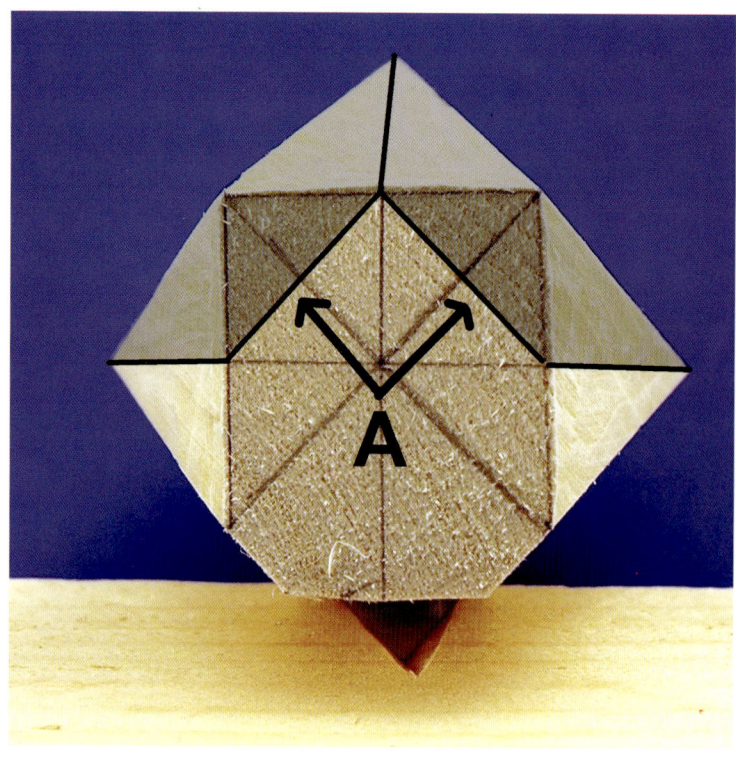

43. Draw in two lines parallel to the outside edges as indicated by (A). These lines will mark the wedge areas as shown in shades. These areas will be removed in the following steps.

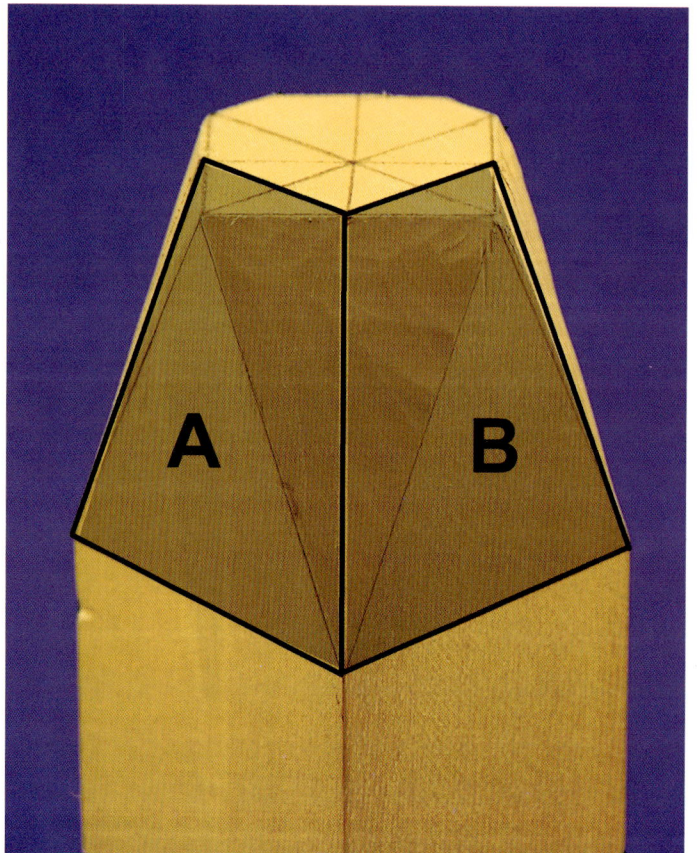

44. View from the back side. By removing the shaded area, as shown by (A) and (B), you will allow for the head to be brought forward so that Mary can have the head appear to be bent slightly in reverence.

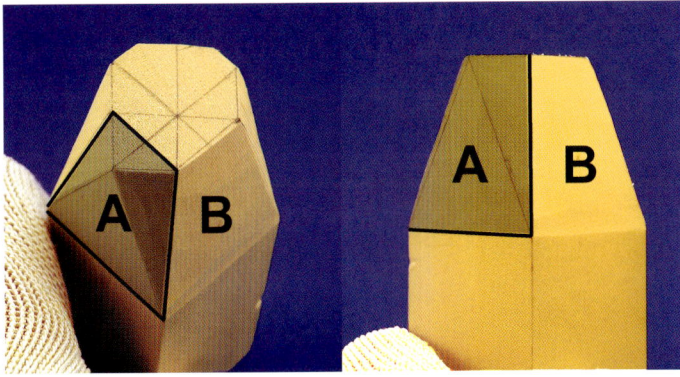

45. Using the knife, remove the wedge as shown in (B). Next, remove the other side (A). You will need to make several passes to remove the wood. Take care to make long flat cuts and avoid rounding the carving.

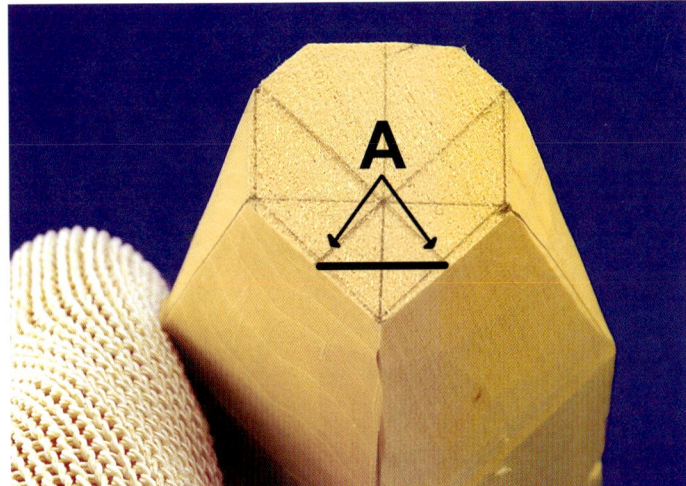

46. Next, draw a line connecting the two lines as shown by (A). This will mark the next area to remove.

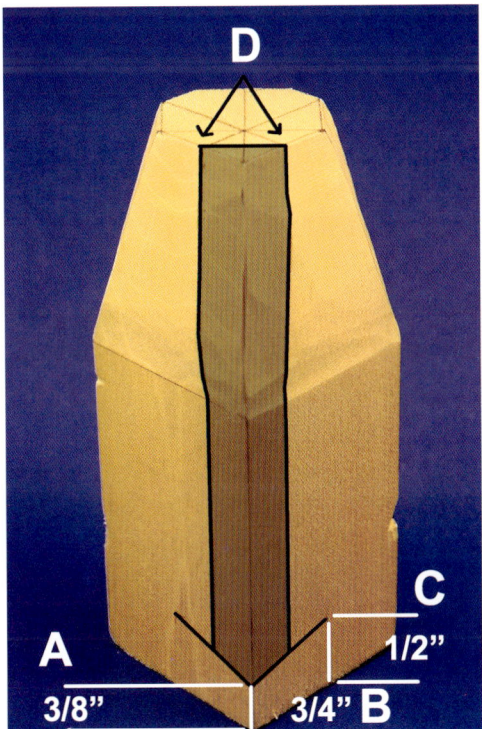

47. Draw a line 3/8 inch from the bottom of the block as shown by (A). Mark a line 3/4 inch from each side from the back edge as shown by (B). Next place a mark 1/2 inch above the 3/4 inch mark (C). Draw a line from (C) to (A) on both sides. Beginning at (D), extend the lines down the back side from the top. This area will be removed. This will reduce the bulk of the carving and allow it to appear less box-like.

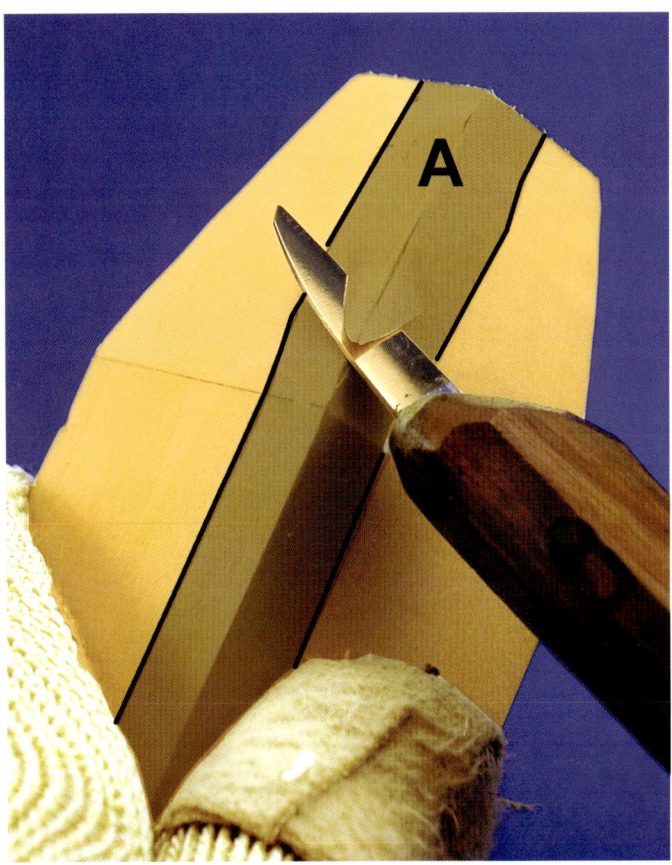

48. Use the knife to remove the wood as indicated by the shaded area.

49. Make a stop cut as shown. You may need to make several cuts to remove the wood. Continue to remove the wood down the back side so that it ends at the stop cut.

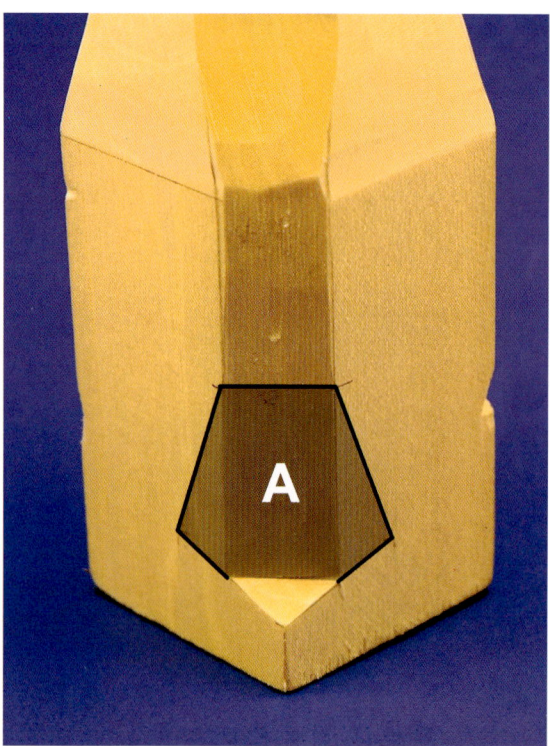

50. Next we need to widen the base of the carving. This will make the Mary figure appear to be kneeling. Remove the wood in the shaded area as show. Again, take long flat cuts and do not round.

52. Using the knife, remove this wedge.

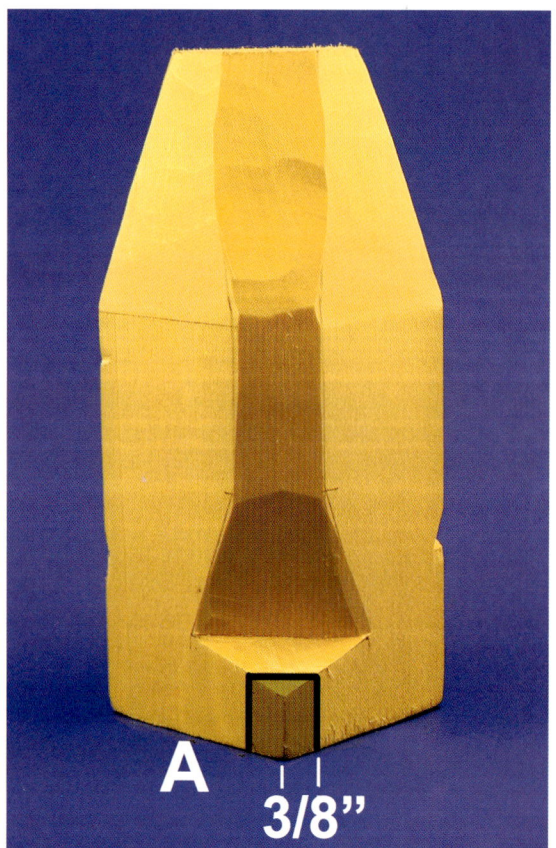

51. Mark off 3/8-inches on both sides of the back as shown. Removal of this wood serves a couple of purposes: one, it helps reduce the blocky look and two, removes the possibility of being broken off by someone inadvertently dropping the carving.

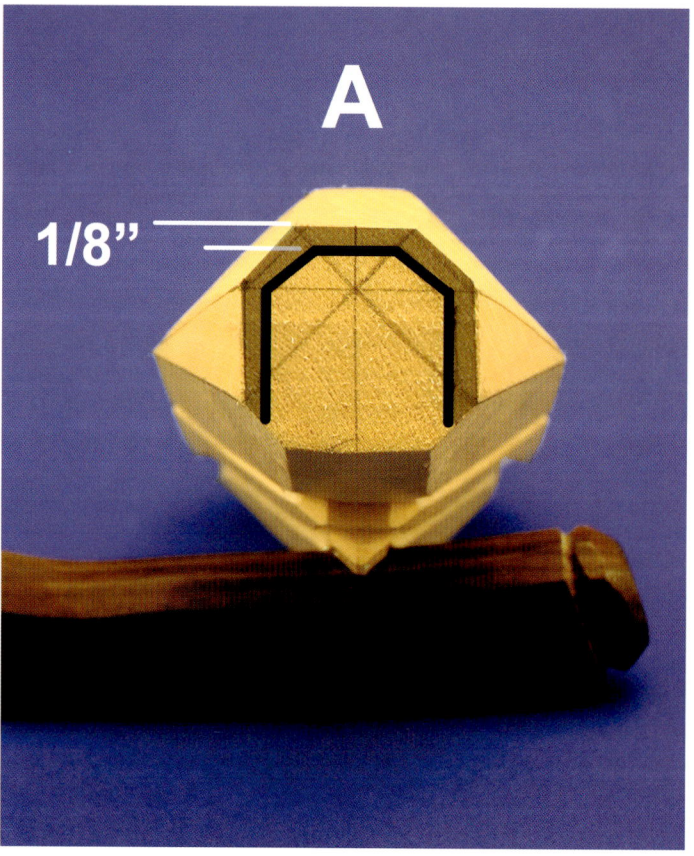

53. Draw parallel lines in 1/8 inch from the outside edge all around the top of the headpiece as shown.

54. Using a knife, start at the shoulder line and remove the wood. Note the long, flat cuts.

56. Using a knife, remove this wedge. A good flat blade knife will make this task easier.

55. Place a mark 3/16 inch below the front of the carving. Extend this line around the sides and end up on the very top of the back as shown in the right hand side of the photo. This taper will further enhance the look that Mary is bent slightly over.

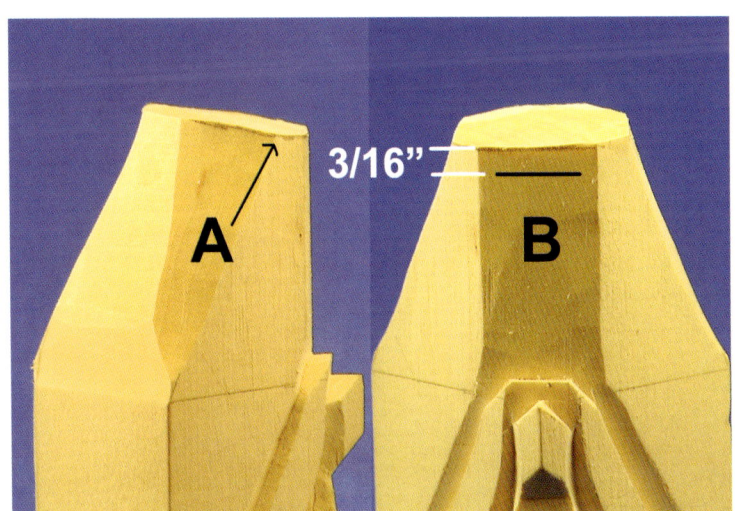

57. Progress so far is shown in (A). Mark another line 3/16 inch below the front as shown in (B). This will be the top of Mary's veil.

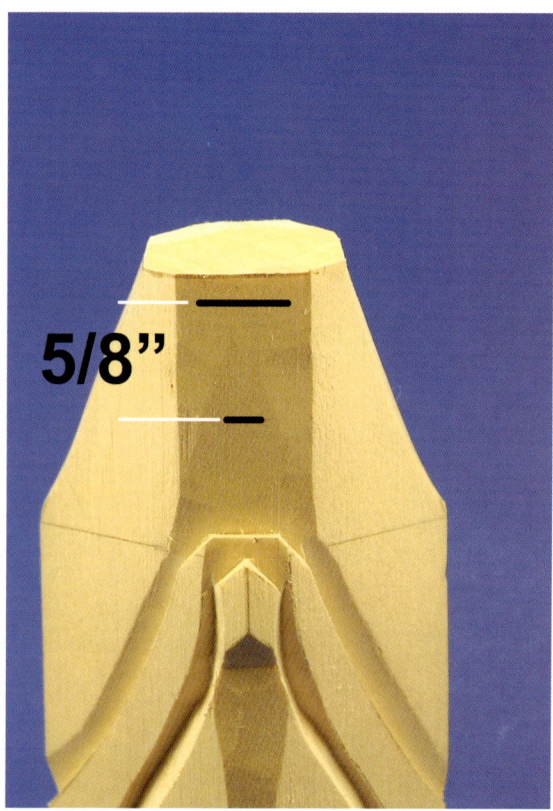

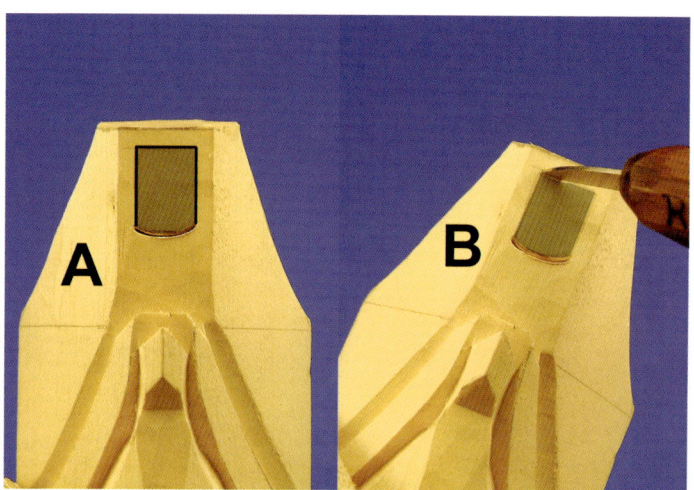

60. Mary's face will be in the shaded area as shown in (A). Using the knife, start at the outside the edge and cut towards the middle as shown in (B). Turn the block over and make the other cut from the outside to the middle. Always cutting toward the middle and stopping at the middle protects you and the carving in the event you slip. The cut should be approximately 1/8 inch deep.

58. Mark a line 5/8 inch below the previous line. This will be the bottom of Mary's face.

59. Using the #7-5/8 inch gouge, make stop cut to set in the bottom of Mary's face.

61. Take the knife and make a stop cut down both sides of the face.

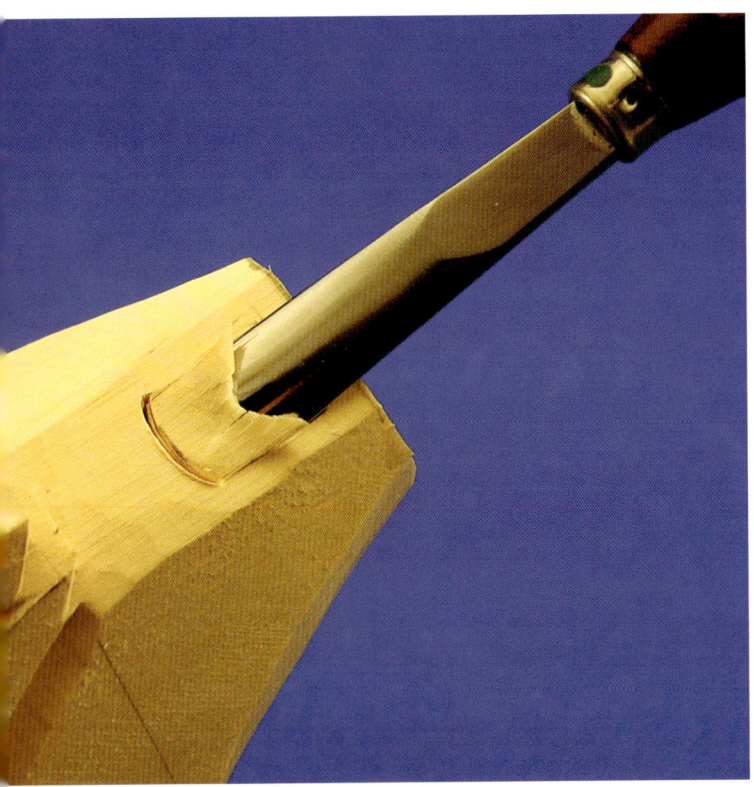

62. Take the #7-5/8 inch gouge and slide it down the front of the face. You will be removing more wood at the base of the face than at the top. Again, this will allow Mary's head to appear to be bent down in reverence.

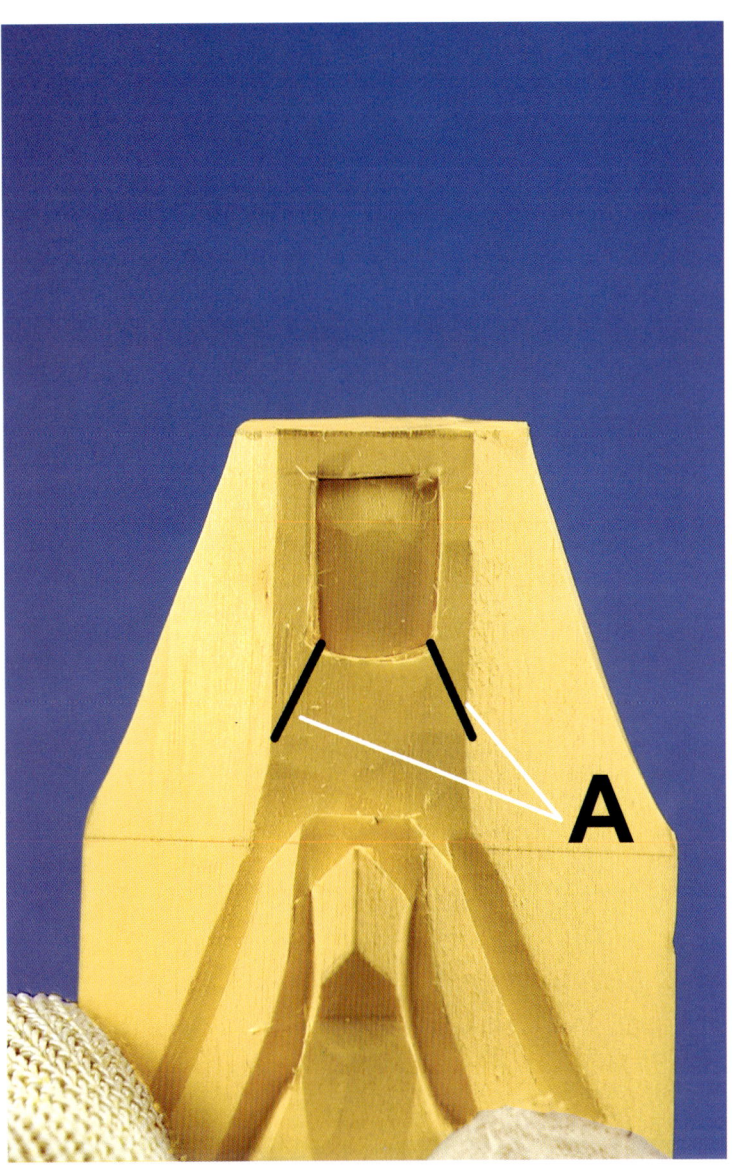

64. Draw two lines as indicated by (A). These will give the appearance of the folds of the veil created by Mary head leaning forward.

63. Take a knife or a #3-1/2 inch gouge and remove the top of the face. This will allow the face to tuck under the veil. Take care to make sure that the forehead is higher than the base of the face.

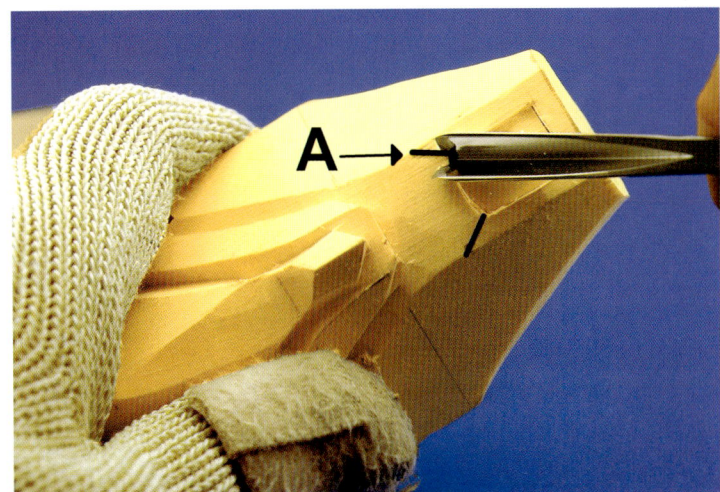

65. Use the V-tool and make the cut to the bottom side of the line and remove the wood. Tilt the V-tool so that one side is lying down towards the front of the carving.

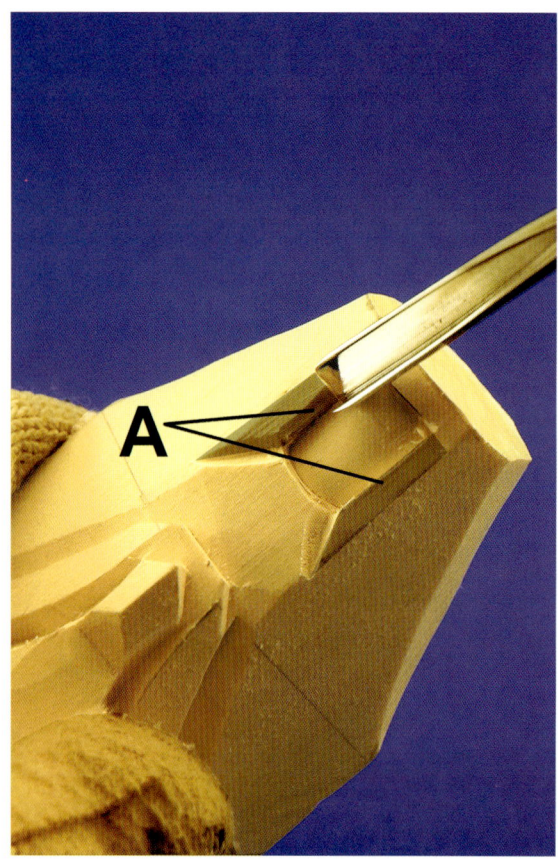

66. Take the V-tool or knife and remove the wood that is shaded (A). This will open the front of the veil.

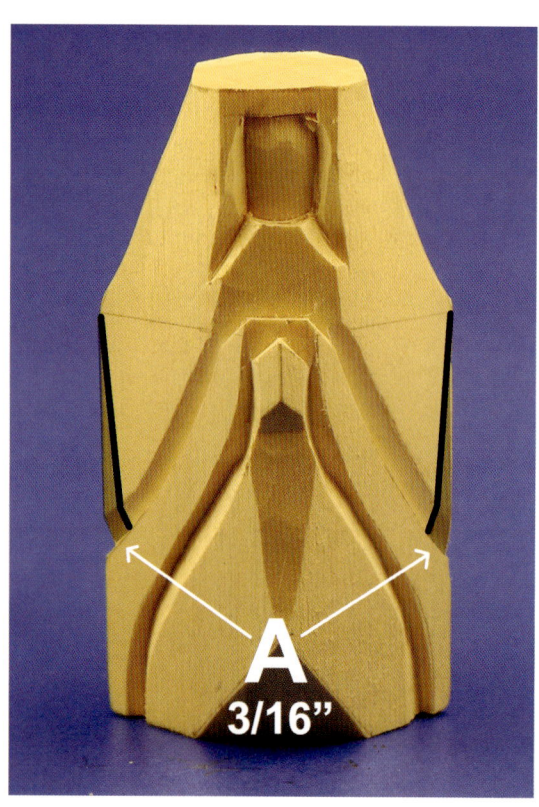

68. Next we need to taper the sides of the robe so that it flows downward and into the top of the opening. Start at the shoulder line and draw a line down to the top of the fold where it hits to the top of the robe. This will be approximately 3/16 inch in at the bottom as shown by (A).

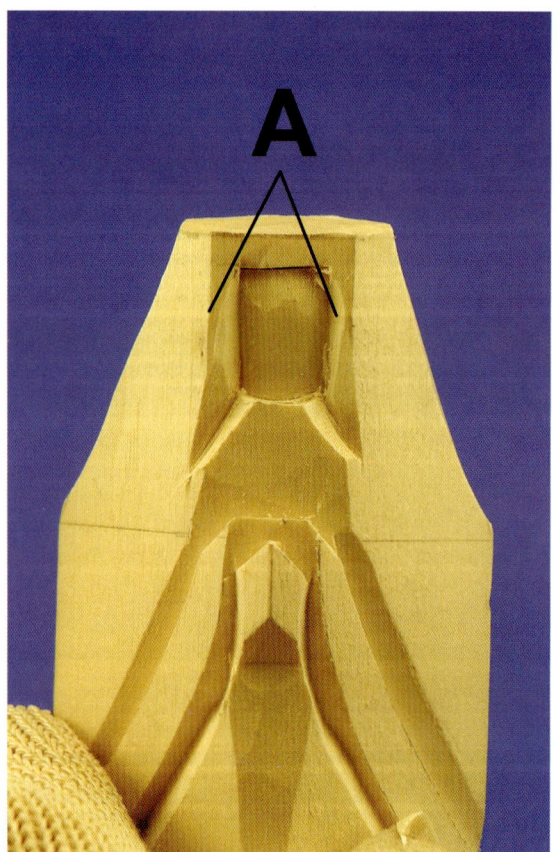

67. Progress so far. Notice how the veil sweeps away from the face as shown in (A).

69. Using the knife, make a stop cut at the 3/16 inch point (as shown in previous photo labeled (A)), remove the wood that is shaded in the photo. Try to make a long flat cut.

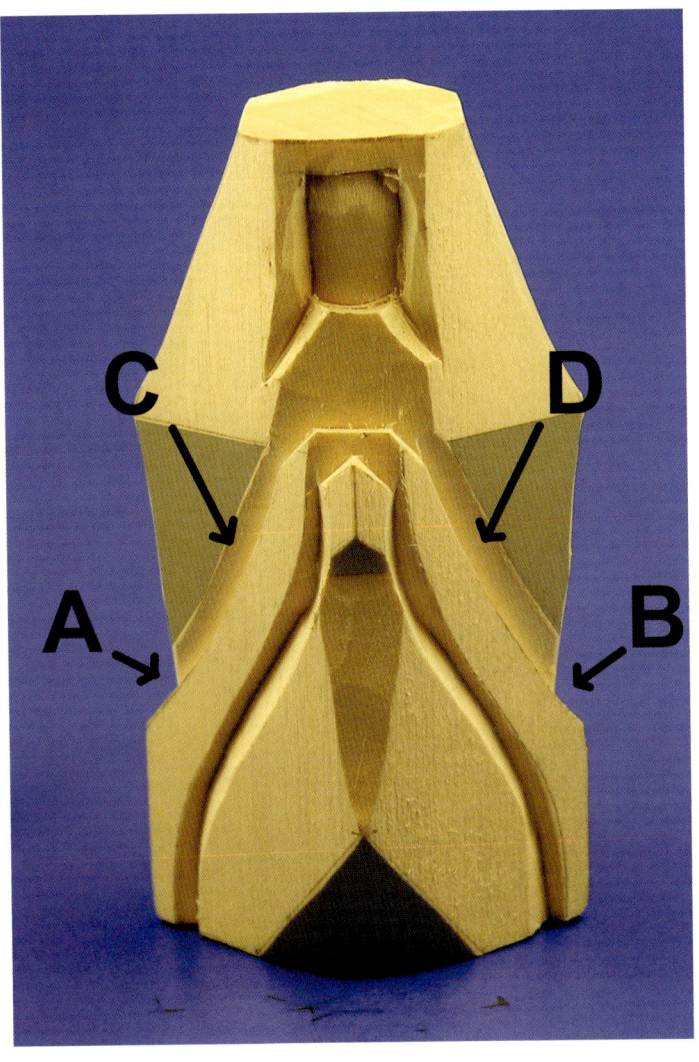

70. Your carving should resemble the photo now. Note how the cloak falls in behind the front part as indicated by (A) and (B). To remove some of the bulkiness, you will need to remove some wood as shown by the arrows indicated by (C) and (D). These cuts will start at the shoulder line and finish at the top of the cloak.

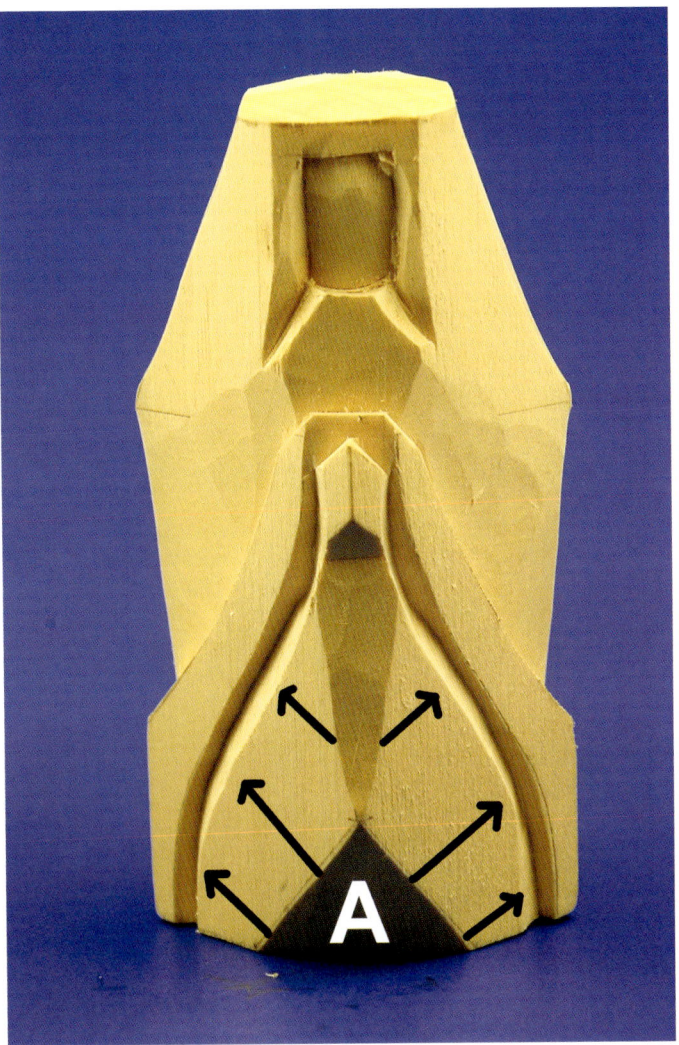

72. The next cuts will reduce the bulkiness of the front of the robe and tuck it under the cloak. The cuts start at the front and go toward the cloak as shown by (A).

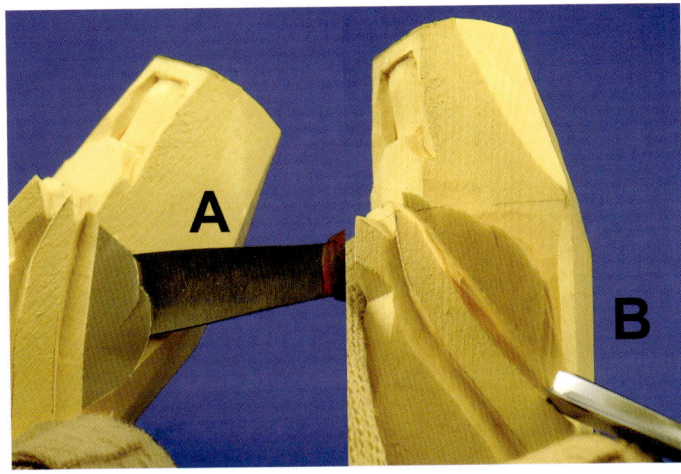

71. Using a #3 gouge or a knife, remove the wood as shown in (A). Take the V-tool and clean up the top of the robe as shown by (B).

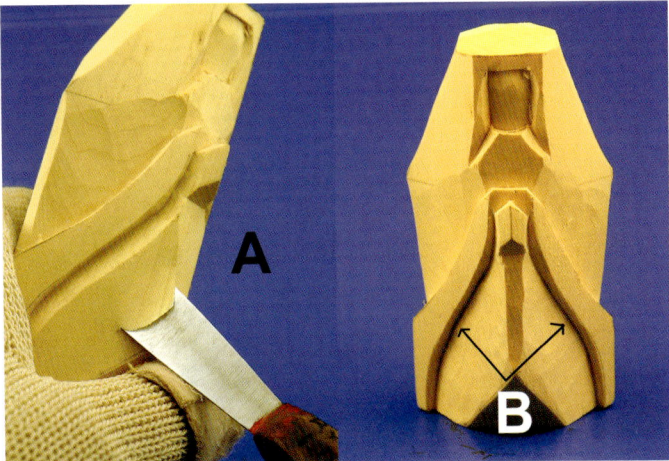

73. Using a #3-1/2 inch gouge or a knife, remove the wood as shown in (A). Take the V-tool and clean up the top of the robe as shown by (B). Since this will have a single color finish, we will need to rely on shadows to accentuate the areas that we want highlighted. To do this will involve undercutting parts of the carving in the next several steps.

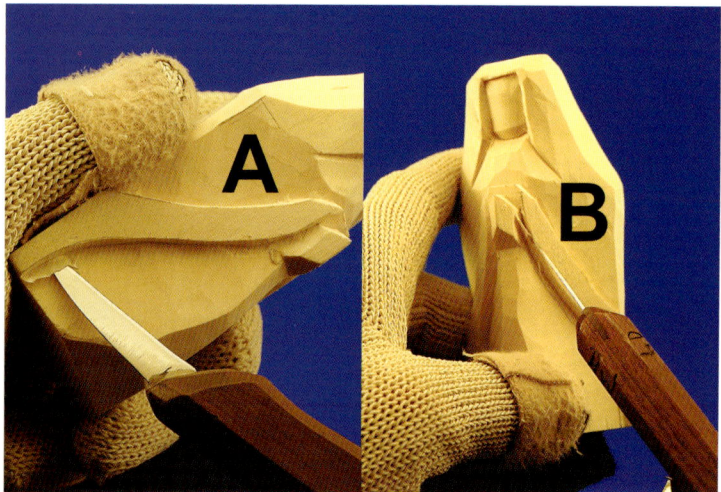

74. Using a knife, lay it flat against the robe as shown by (A) and make a cut along the robe until you reach the hands. Take the knife and make a cut perpendicular to the robe as shown in (B). Take your time and make a single cut to remove the small sliver of wood that should fall away.

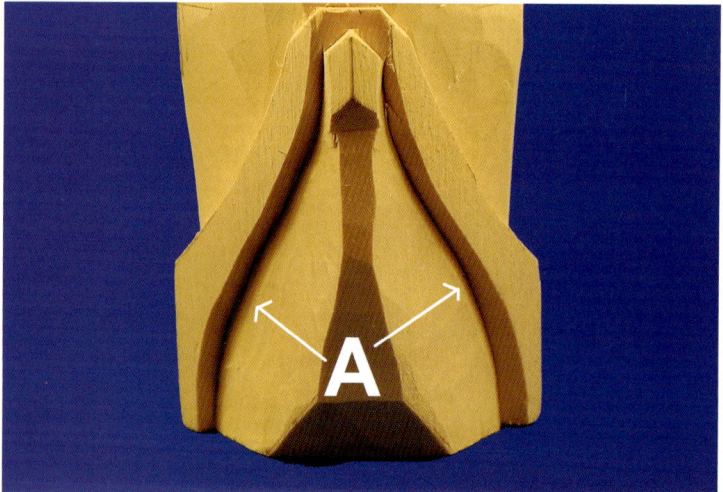

75. Progress so far. Note the prominent shadows as shown by (A).

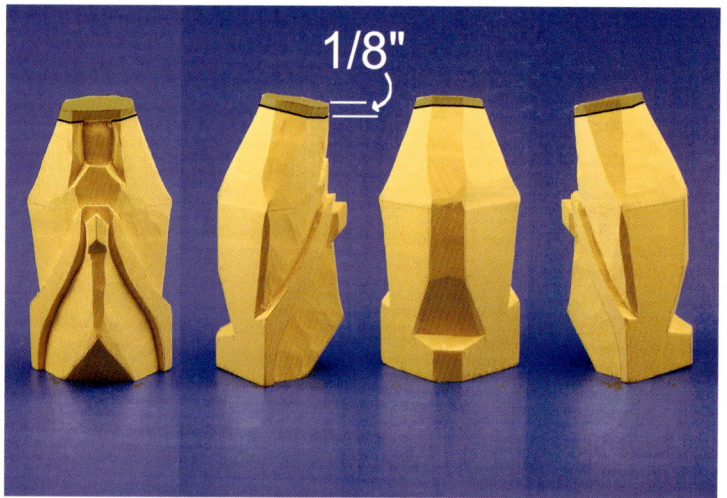

76. Next, we will need to taper the top of the veil over Mary's head. To do this, mark down 1/8 inch all the around the top of the carving as shown.

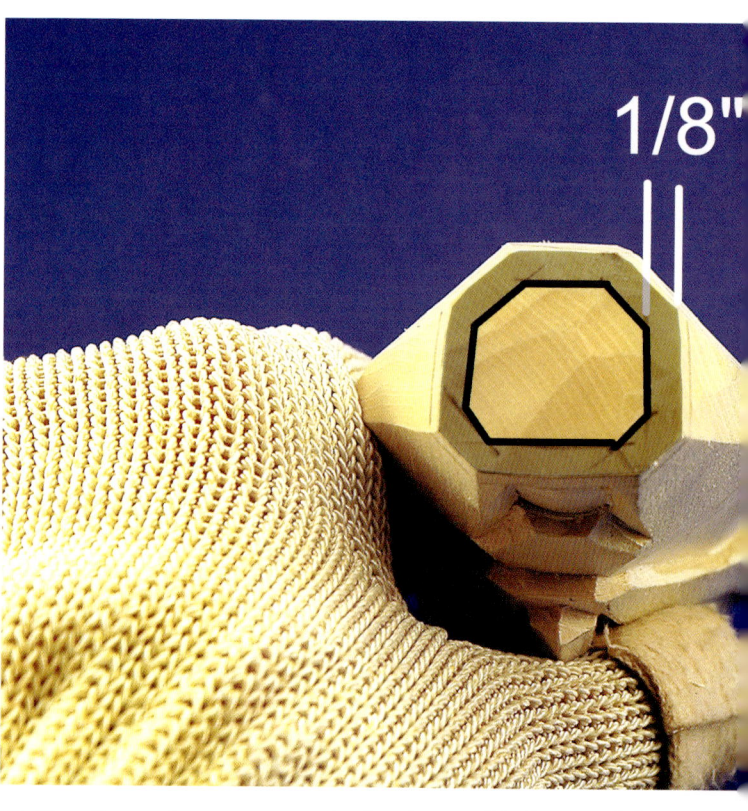

77. Turn the carving so you are viewing the top. Mark a parallel line 1/8 inch from the outside edge, all the way around the top as shown.

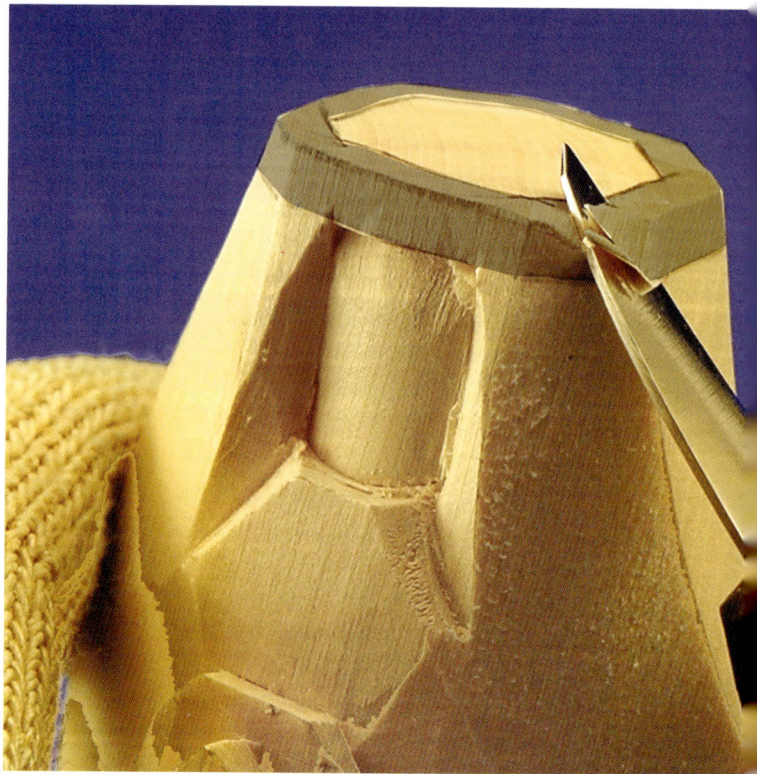

78. Using a knife, remove the wood between the two lines drawn in the previous steps. This will provide a 45-degree angle transition.

79. Next, to widen up the veil and also enhance the flow of the front, use a knife to make the cut shown to remove the wood that is shaded.

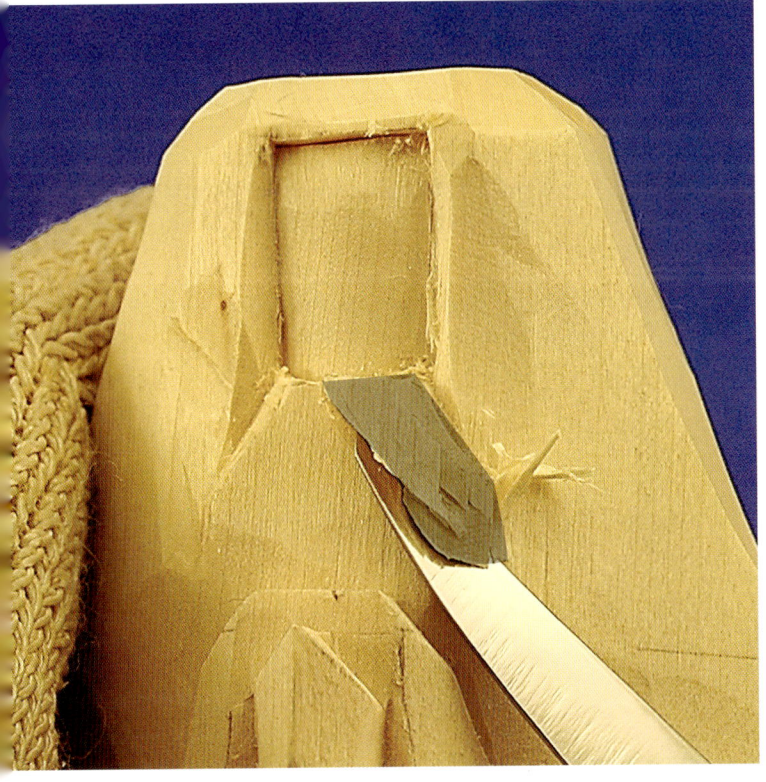

80. Remove the wedge by using the knife and cutting towards the veil as shown. Do this on both sides.

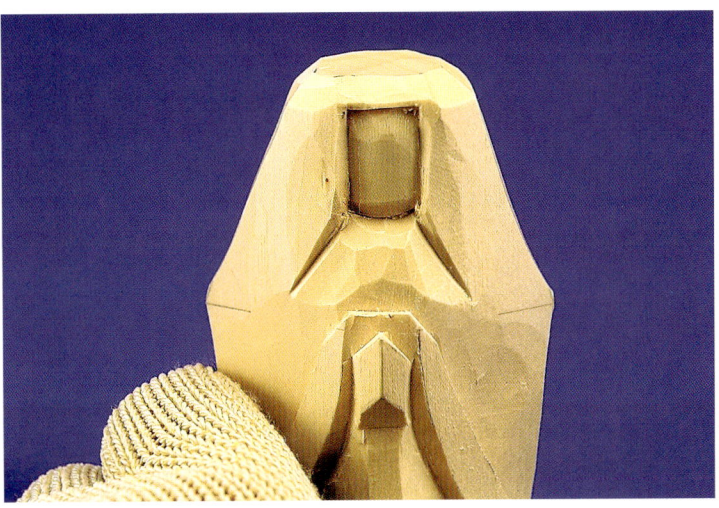

81. Progress so far. Look over the carving and remove any areas that contain slivers of wood. In addition, make sure you have nice flat planes and have not rounded the areas. To soften the hard sharp corners, I use a piece of worn out 220 to 320-grit paper and lightly sand the carving. This will provide for a hand worn or rubbed look when we apply the finish.

82. The front and right sides of the carving of Mary.

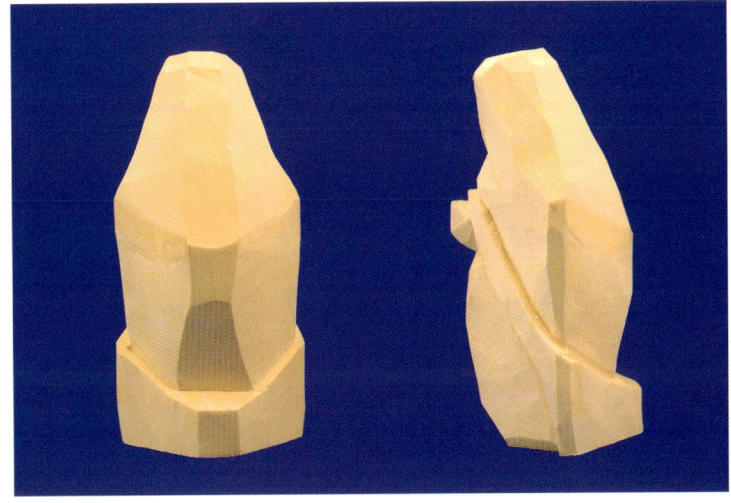

83. The back and left sides of the carving of Mary.

Chapter Two
Joseph

As mentioned previously, once you have mastered the basic cuts, the other remaining pieces of the nativity are variations of the carving of Mary.

To carve Joseph, you will need a 2 inch by 2 inch by 5-3/4 inch block of Basswood. This will allow Joseph to be slightly taller than Mary, thereby creating the illusion that while similar, they are two different pieces. The first step is to establish the shoulder line as shown below.

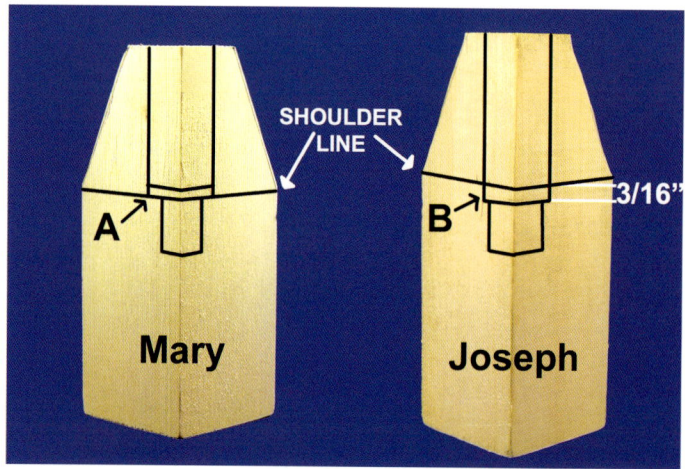

2. Your carving should resemble (B). Notice the difference between Mary's robe covering her hands in (A) and Joseph's robe covers his hands in (B). Mary's robe is 1/8 inch above the shoulder line while Joseph's robe extends 3/16 inch below the shoulder line.

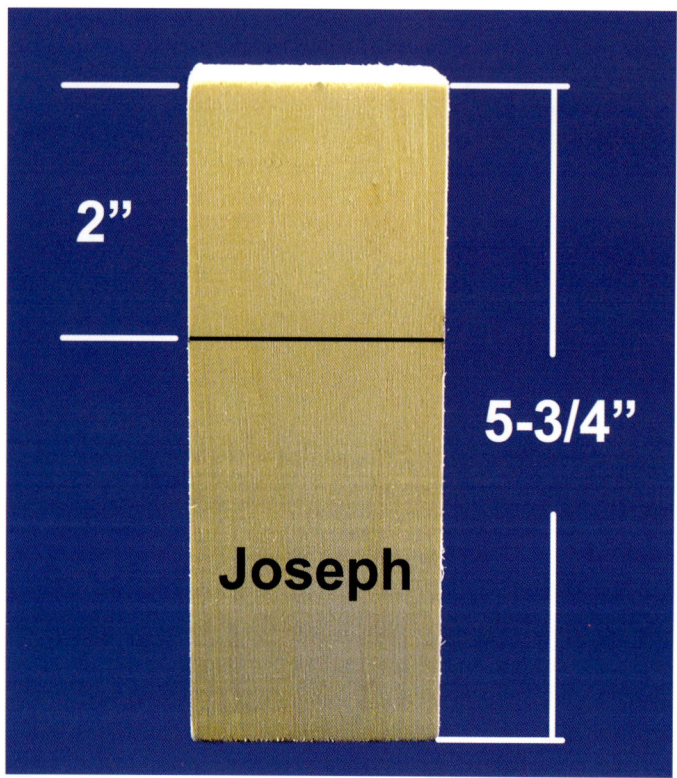

1. Using a ruler, mark a line two inches from the top and continue this line around the block. Alternatively, you can use another 2 inch block for a reference, as in step one of carving Mary.

Since there are quite a few pieces that will be covered in this book and just so much room for photos, I have taken the liberty of just covering the differences in the carvings in comparison to Mary. To carve Joseph, please refer to Steps 1-14 in the first chapter, Flat Plane Carving – Mary.

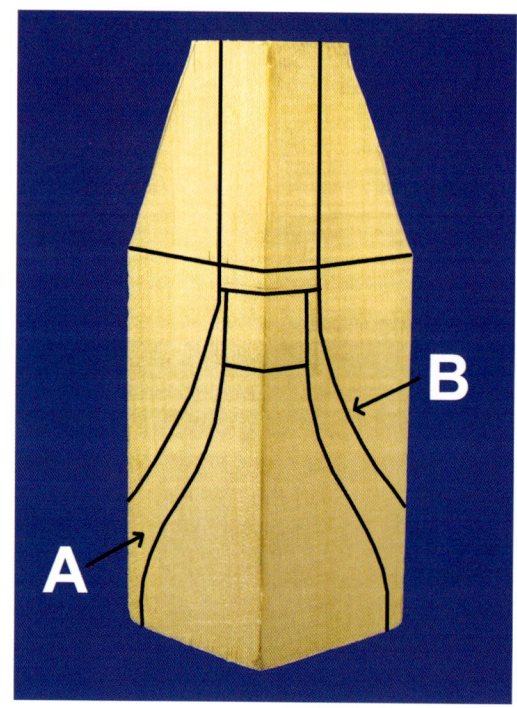

3. The inside and the outside of the robe have a gentle curve flowing from the top of the hands to the base. You can draw these lines in free hand or use the template that is supplied.

Refer to steps 17-54 in the chapter Flat Plane Carving – Mary.

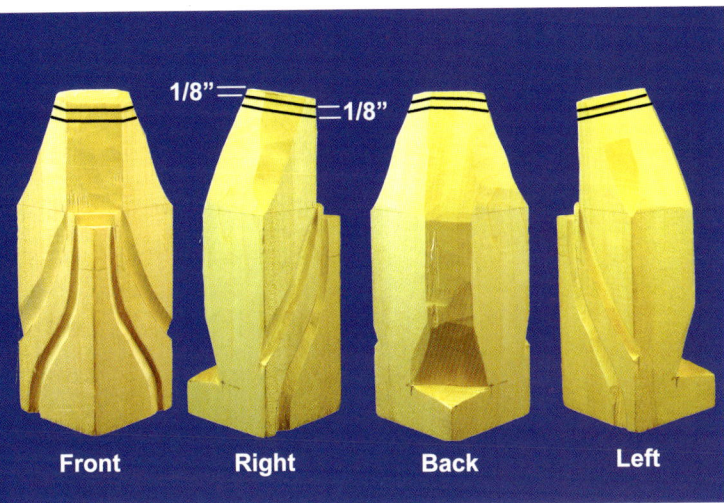

Front   **Right**   **Back**   **Left**

1/8"   1/8"

4. Your carving should resemble the photo shown. Joseph will have a band around his head covering. Mark off 1/8 inch below the top of the carving to indicate the top of the band. Mark another line 1/8 inch below the top of the band to indicate the bottom of the band. Draw this line all the way around the headpiece.

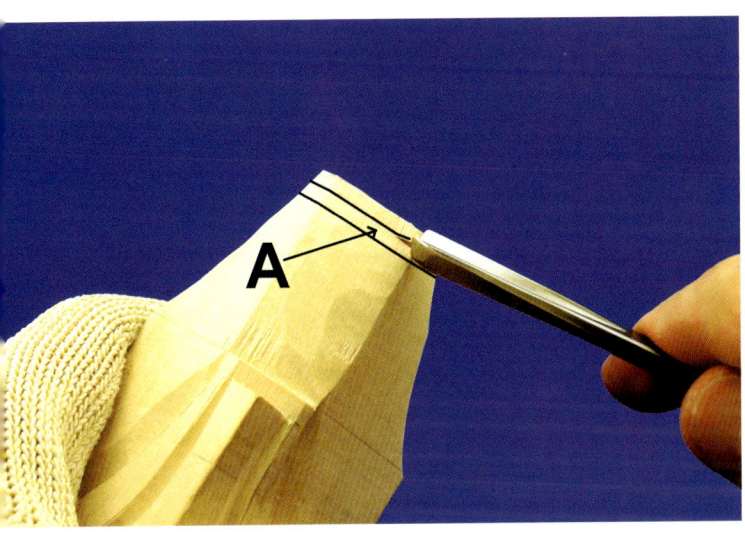

A

5. Take the V-tool and tilt it away from the band and remove the top line as shown in (A).

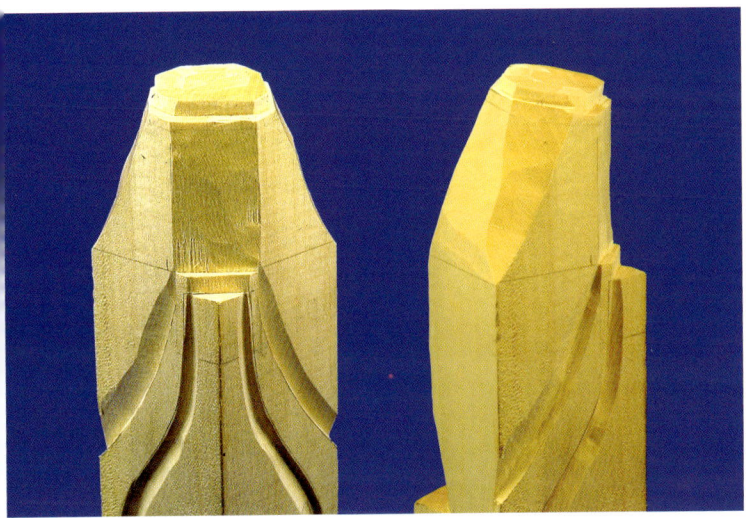

6. Progress so far, front and right hand side.

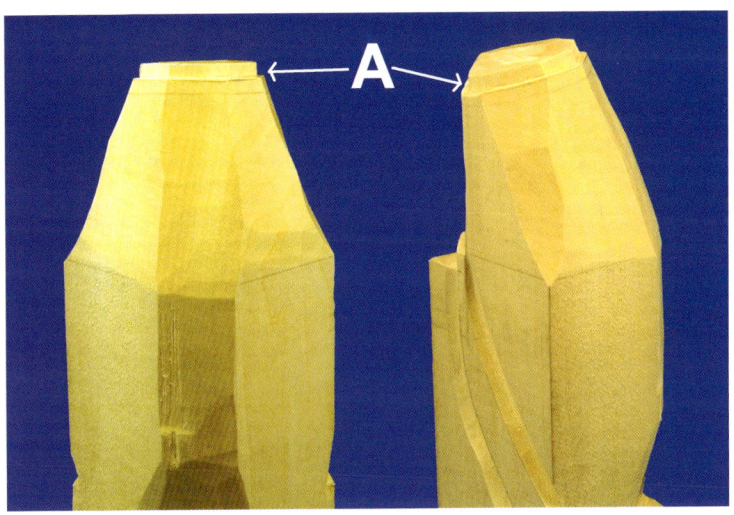

A

7. Progress so far, back and left hand side. Note the step as indicated by (A). You will soften this later.

8. Take the V-tool and tilt it away from the band and remove the bottom line as shown.

5/8"

9. Place a mark 5/8 inch below the bottom of the headband. Refer to Step 57 to 61 of Chapter One -- Mary.

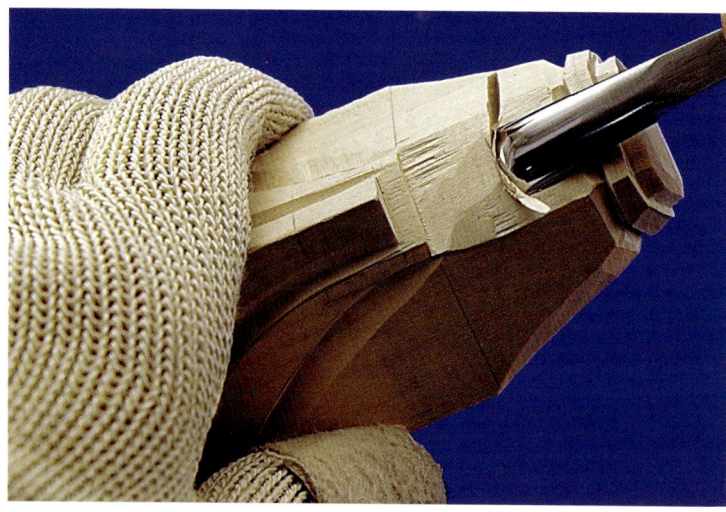

10. Using the #7-5/8 inch gouge, make a cut on this mark. This will indicate the bottom of Joseph's face.

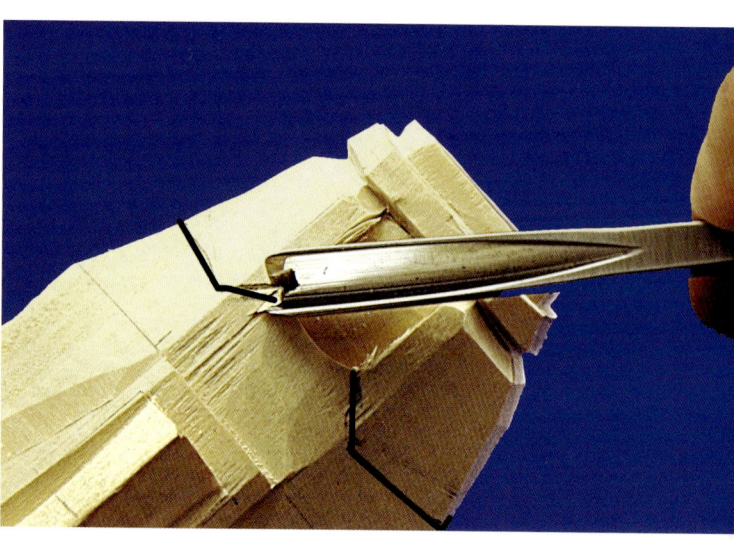

13. Take the V-tool, tilt it away from the head covering and remove the line all the way around that you drew in the previous steps.

11. Joseph's head covering is separate from his cloak. Mark a line 1 inch from the bottom of the band. Continue this line around the top of the carving.

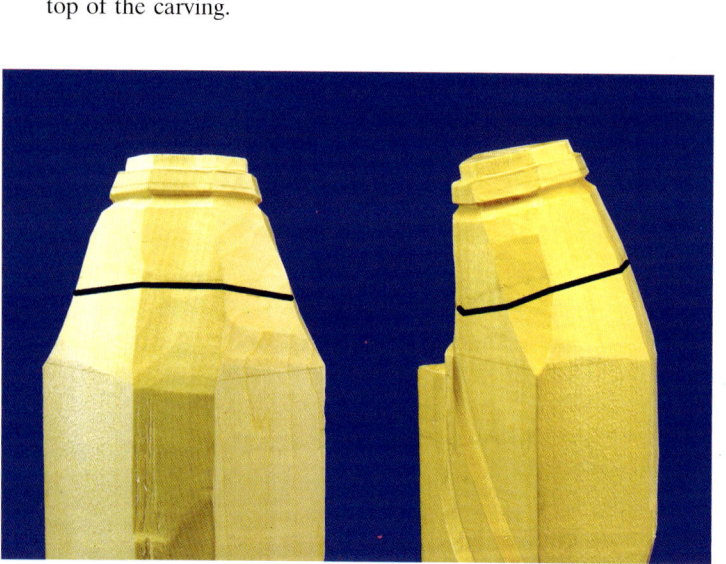

12. The head covering should rise slightly in the back as shown in the photo. This will allow for the appearance that the head is bowed slightly.

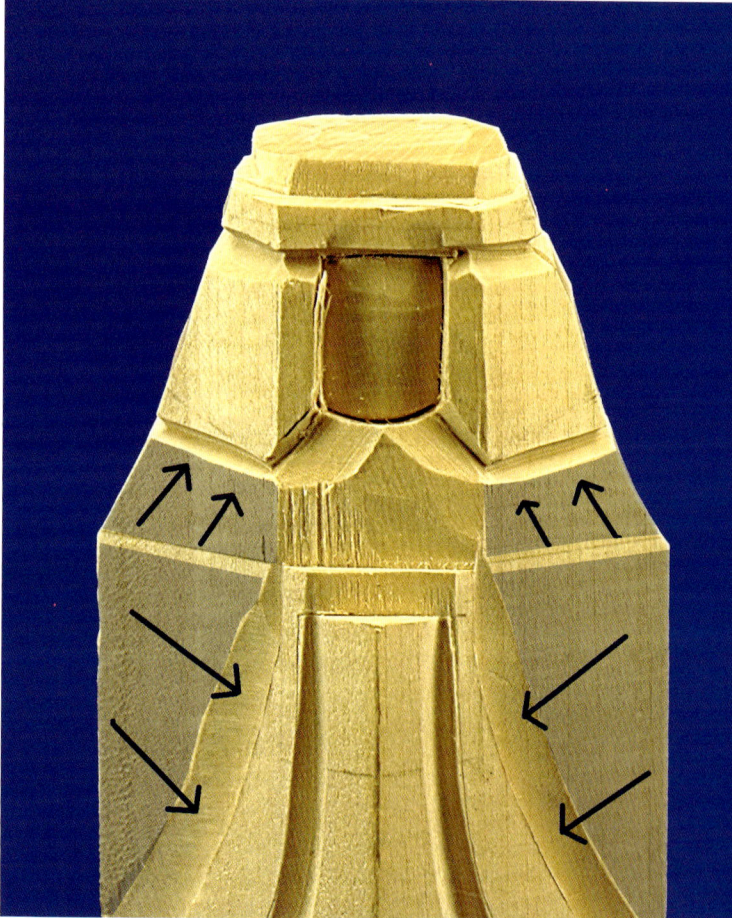

14. Next we will remove the wood that is shaded in the photo. Using a #3-1/2 inch gouge or a knife, remove the wood (shaded) starting at the shoulder and going to the robe and the head covering. This tapers (high) from the shoulder to (low) where it connects to the robe.

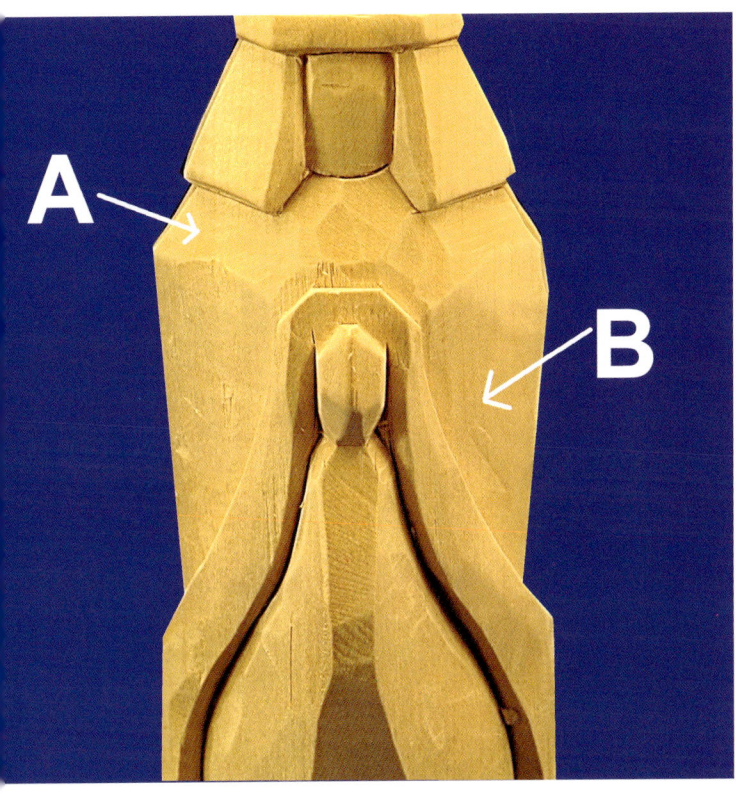

15. Progress so far. Note how the robe flows under the head covers (A) as well as the section of the robe the covers Joseph's hand (B).

17. Clean up the area under Joseph's face by tapering the high part from the hands to the bottom of the face.

16. If the head covering appears to be a little thick, taper the side further as shown in the photo.

18. Taper the top of the head covering by removing a small 45 degree wedge from the top as shown in the photo.

19. Progress so far for Joseph's head covering.

Refer to steps 68 – 75 in the Chapter One – Mary

20. The front and right side of the carving of Joseph. Using a worn out piece of 220 to 320 grit sandpaper, rub down the carving. Take care not to sand too hard and remove the details. You want the carving to look hand worn.

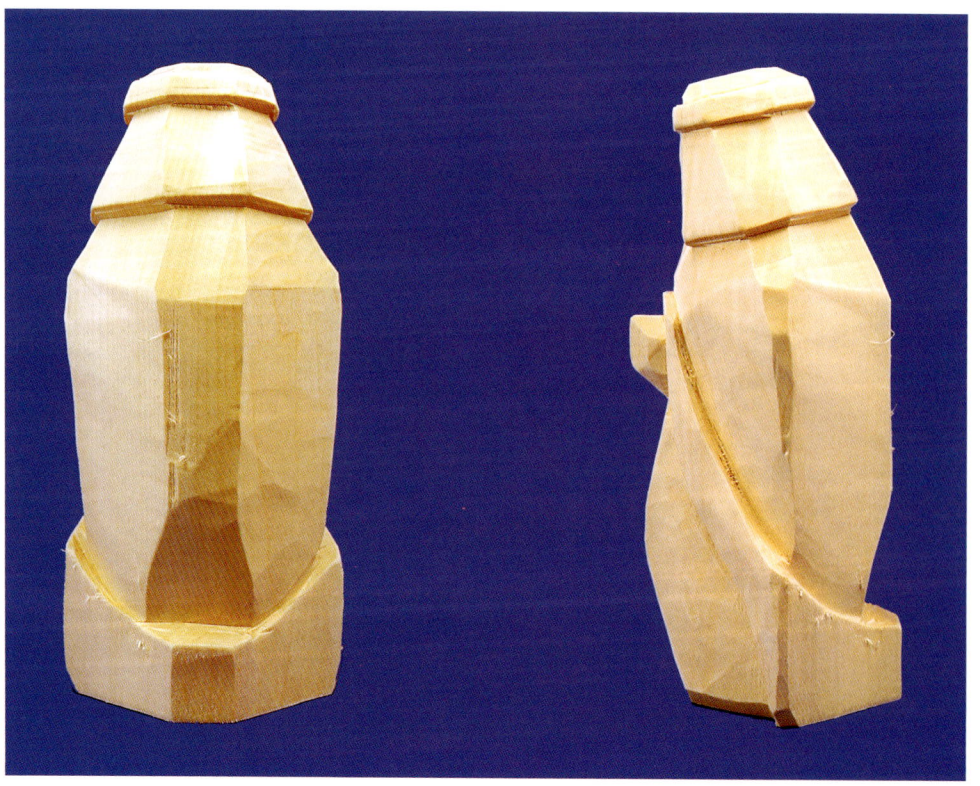

21. The back and left side of the carving of Joseph.

Chapter Three
Crib

When designing the crib, I wanted to make the design as simple as possible and leave the imagery to the person viewing the baby. The result is the crib you will be carving in the following steps.

You will need a 1-1/2 inch by 1-1/2 inch by 2 inch block of Basswood to carve the crib. (Note the grain runs the length of the block.) The first step is to lay out the base of the crib.

3. Using a hand saw or band saw, make the cuts on the lines drawn in the previous steps. Your blank should look like the one shown.

1. Using a ruler, mark a line 5/8 inch from the outside edge. Mark another line 5/8 inch above the base as shown in the photo.

4. Using the knife, make a stab cut *gently* in-between the legs of the crib. The piece of wood should pop out. Be very careful as to not break off a leg while making this cut. If you do, you can glue it back on and continue.

2. Using a ruler, mark a line 5/8 inch from the end. Mark another line 5/8 inch above the base as shown in the photo.

5. Now, take a knife and make a stab cut gently in-between the end of the legs of the crib. The piece of wood should pop out. Note: if you push too hard and cut off the leg, glue it back on and continue.

7. Mark a line 3/16 inch all the way around the top of the block of wood as shown.

6. Progress of the crib so far.

Baby Jesus will be laying inside the crib, so we will need to lay out the top side to include the wrapped baby as well as delineate the outside of the crib.

8. Make a top cut approximately 1/8 inch deep and cut halfway across the top of the block as shown in the photo. Turn the block around and make a cut from the opposite corner to the middle. This method removes the possibility of the knife slipping and cutting past the end or, worse, cutting you. Do this all the way around the top.

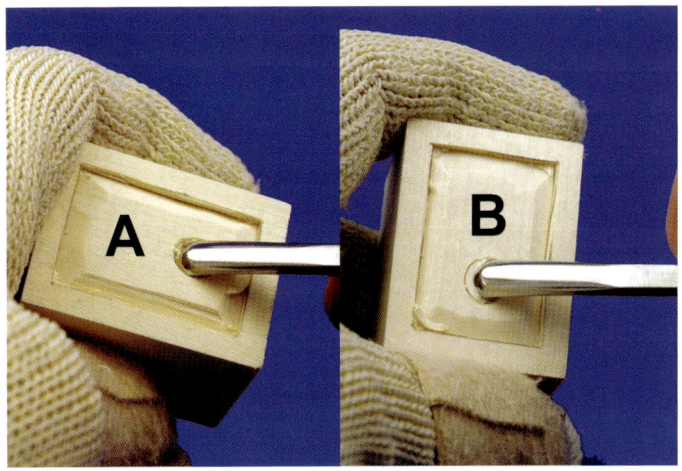

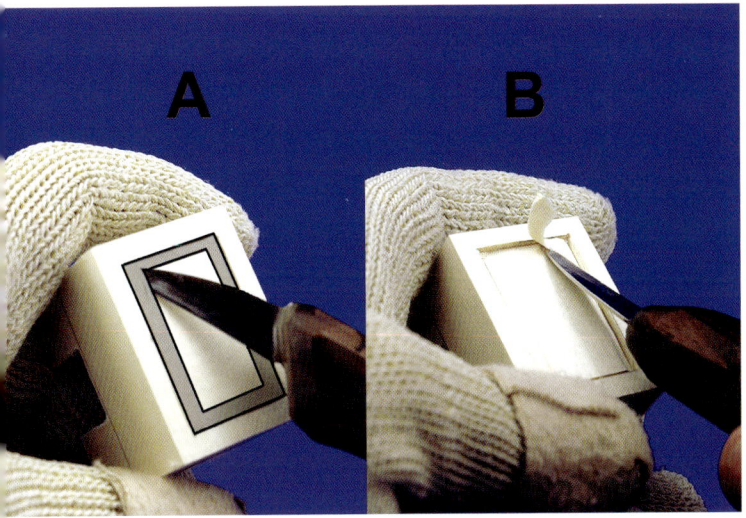

9. To obtain the appearance of the blanket being tucked into the crib, we will need to remove a small wedge of wood as shown by the shaded area by (A). Using a knife, make a cut to remove the small wedge as shown in (B).

11. You may want to practice this step on a scrap piece of wood before making the cuts in the crib. Take the #7-3/8 inch gouge, lay it flat (round side up) and start at the middle of the mark which is the center of the face, remove the wood as shown in (A). Now take the same gouge and come across the grain as shown in (B). You may need to make several cuts until a small dome appears.

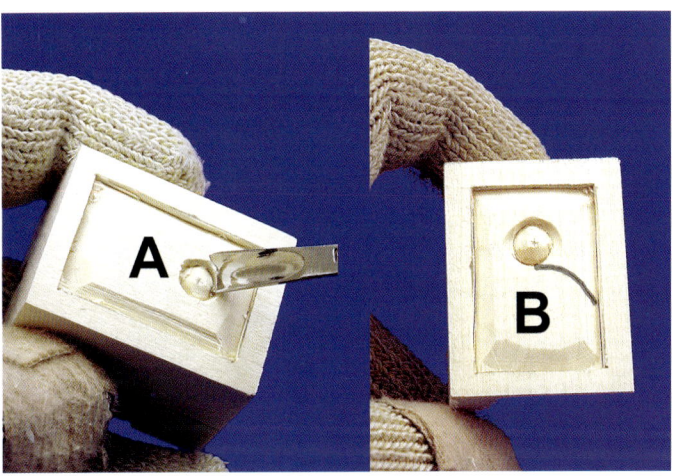

12. Using the gouge, deepen the edge around the face in (B). Draw an arc from the bottom of the face to the side of the crib. This will represent the blanket being tucked in.

10. Place a mark 3/4 inch from one end and 3/4 inch from the outside edge as shown. This will be the center of baby Jesus' face.

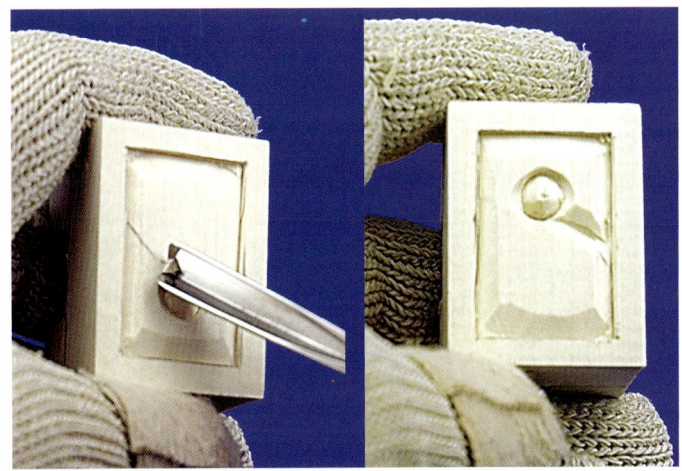

13. Take the V-tool and remove the line you drew in the previous step as shown in the left side of the photo. Your crib should look like the crib shown in the right side of the photo.

14. To add more to the effect of the blanket wrapping baby Jesus, we will deepen the corners by remove the wood as shown in the photo.

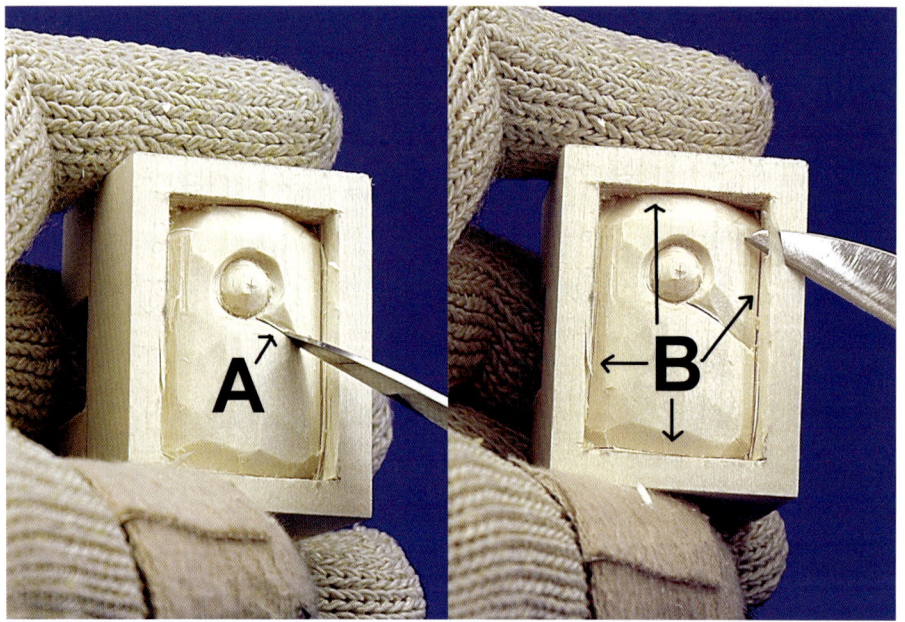

15. Take the knife and cut down the line of the blanket fold (A). This will allow the finish to go into this area and darken. This will add to the shadow effect. Remove the sharp edges of the inside of the crib by removing a small wedge along the inside as shown in (B).

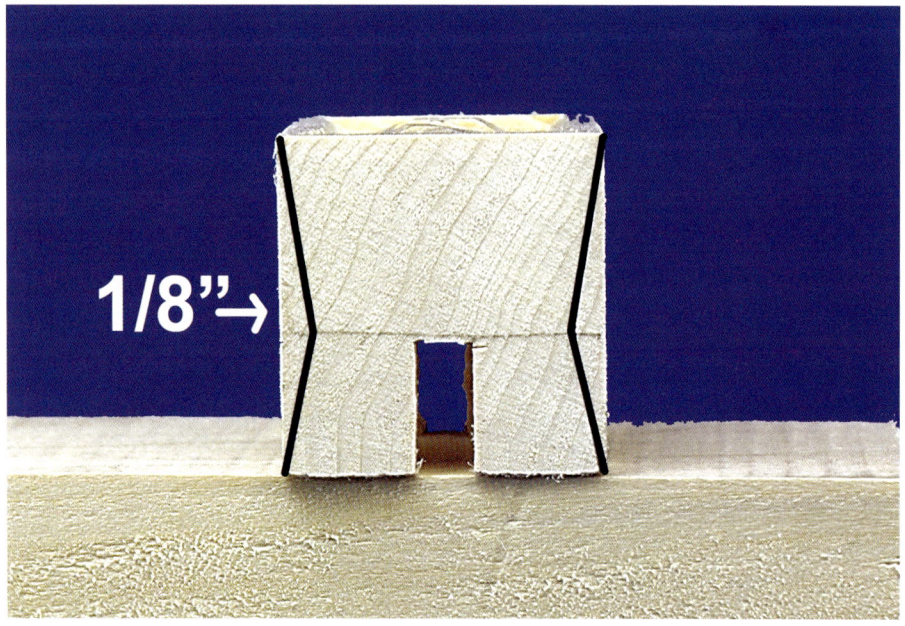

1/8"→

16. Using a ruler, locate a point 1/8 inch in from the sides at the 5/8 inch mark that you drew in steps 1 and 2. Draw lines from the top and the bottom to this mark. You will be removing this wood to give the appearance that the crib is tapered on the sides.

17. Using the knife, remove the wood from the base of the feet to the 5/8 inch mark as shown in the left photo. Use the knife or a #3 gouge to remove the wood along the sides as shown.

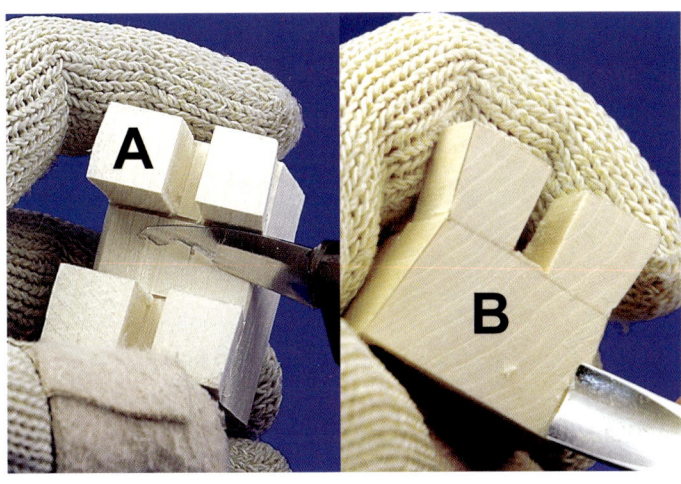

18. Now is a good time to clean up the bottom area of the crib as shown in (A). Take a #7-5/8 inch or equivalent gouge and remove the saw marks on the edge grain. Make small cuts to simulate that the blocks were hand hewn as shown in (B).

20. You may want to deepen the edges of the crib and round over the blanket to get a more 3-D look. Using a worn out piece of 220 to 320 grit sandpaper, rub down the carving. Take care not to sand too hard and remove the details. You want the carving to look hand worn.

19. Continue this around the crib. Your crib should look like one in the photo.

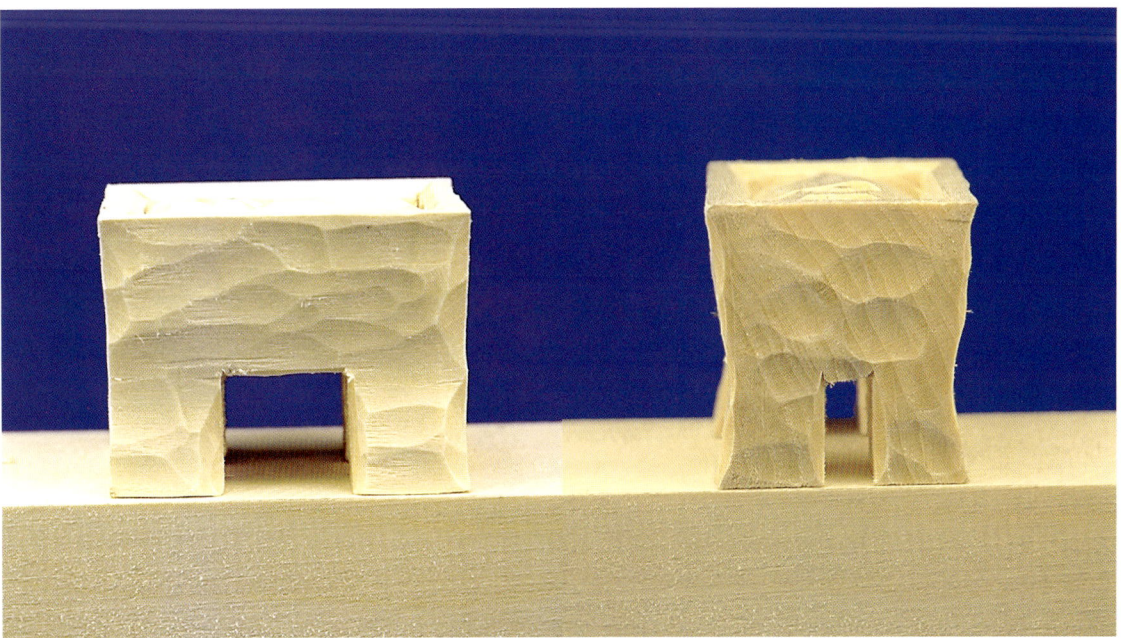

Chapter Four
Shepherd

Once you have mastered the basic cuts, the other remaining pieces of the nativity are variations of the carving of Mary or Joseph.

To carve the shepherd, you will need a 2 inch by 2 inch by 6 inch block of Basswood. This will allow the shepherd to stand and be slightly taller than Joseph. The shepherd differs from Joseph and Mary in that it will have a blanket or large shawl over his head and will have both hands holding a staff. The first step is to establish the shoulder line.

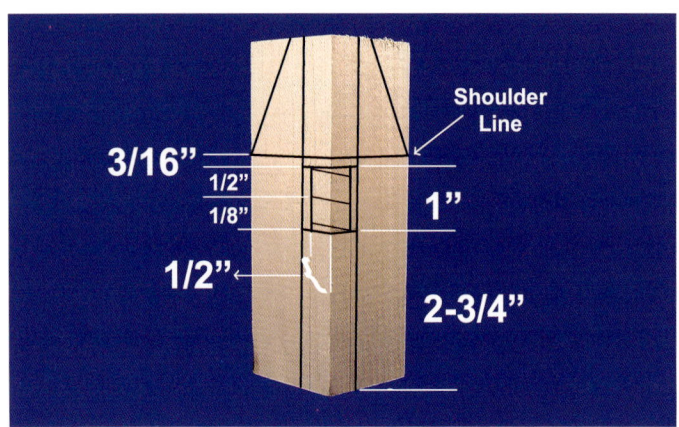

1. Using a ruler, lay out the lines as shown in the photo. The bottom of the hands are 2-3/4 inch above the base and 1 inch in height. The width of the hands measures 1/2 inch from the front edge and will have a slight taper. The top of the hands and robe are 3/16 inch below the shoulder line.

Refer to steps in the first chapter, Flat Plane Carving – Mary.

2. The shepherd is standing, so we will need to remove the wood along the back side all the way to the base. Place a mark 3/4 inch above the base and draw a line to the end of the block. Use a knife and remove the wood that is shaded.

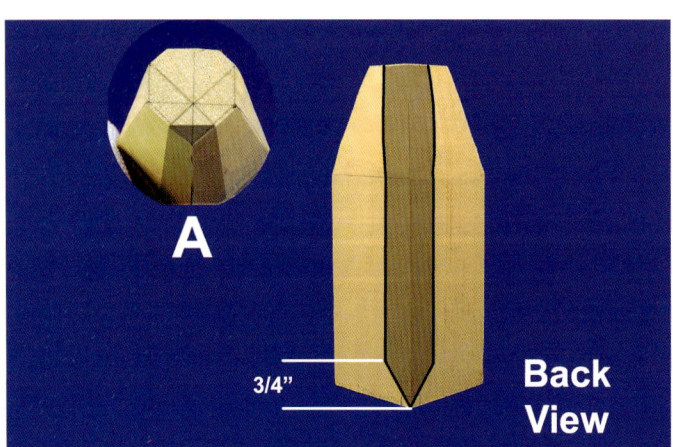

3. Place a mark 3/16 inch down on the front of the face. Place another mark 3/4 inch below that to mark the end of the face. Using a #7-5/8 inch or equivalent gouge, set in the face of the shepherd. Refer to Steps 57 to 63 in Chapter One -- Mary.

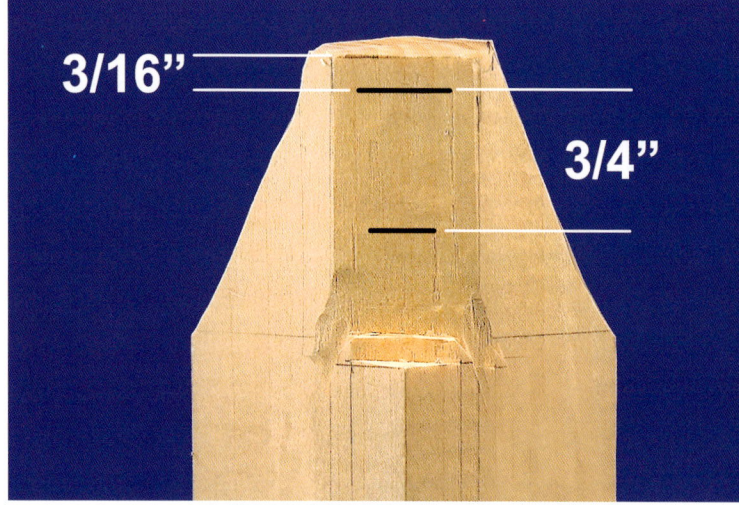

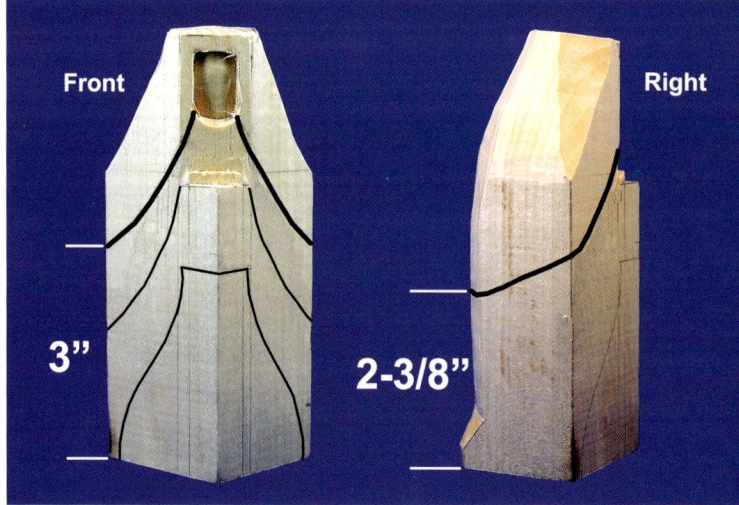

4. Place a mark 3-inches from the bottom on each side of the block as shown in the left photo. Draw a gentle arc from the corner of the face area to this mark as shown in the left hand photo. Place a mark 2-3/8 inch from the bottom on the back of the block as shown. Continue a gentle sweeping arc from each side to this mark.

5. Continue a gentle sweeping arc from each side to this mark. Try to balance the arc across the back of the block.

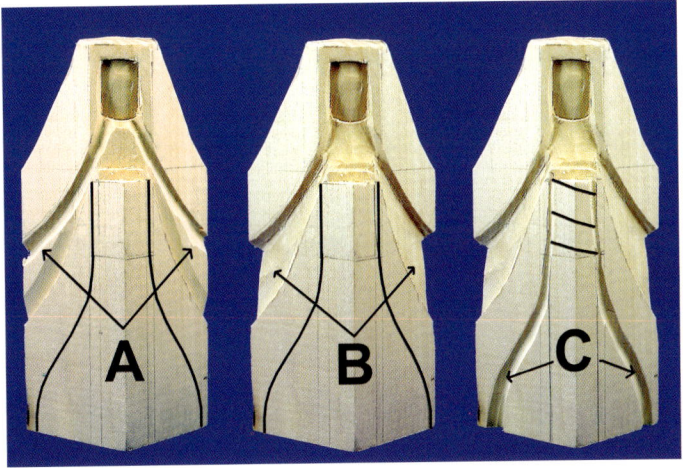

6. Using the V-tool, turn the tool so that one edge is perpendicular to the head covering as shown in (A). Using the knife or a #3 gouge, remove the wood between the head covering and the cloak as shown in (B). Use the V-tool, turning the tool so that one edge is perpendicular to the cloak as shown in (C).

7. The wood, as indicated by the arrows in (A), will need to be removed. This will allow the robe to tuck under the head covering. Using a knife or #3 gouge, remove the wood as shown in (B). Taper the cut from the bottom to the head covering. In the next step, you will be drilling a hole in the hands to hold the shepherd's staff. Take your time to plan the placement of the staff. It works best if the staff is at a slight angle, so as not to hide the face and appear to be more natural. *Use care and caution as you drill the hole into the hands so as not to cause the bit to bind and have the wood block spin freely.*

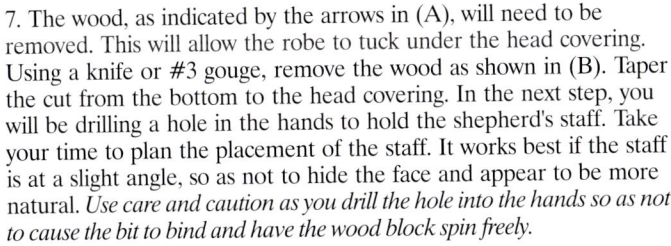

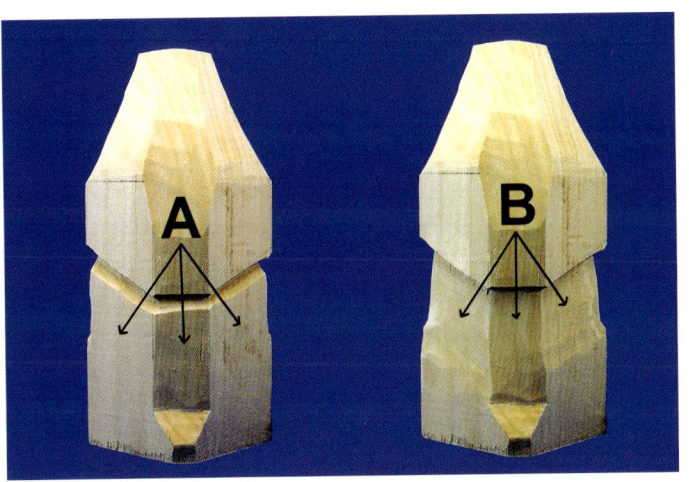

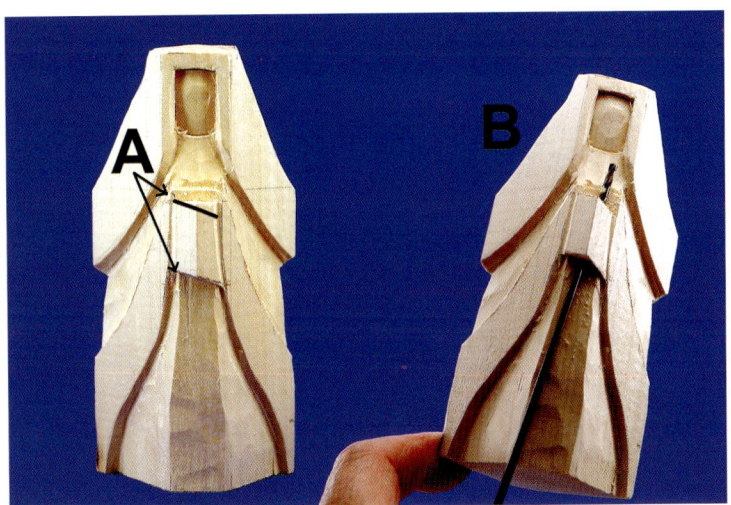

8. Remove the wedge above and below the hands as shown in (A). Mount the block into a suitable work holder (take care not to damage the wood in the work holder) and using the six inch 3/16 inch drill bit, drill a hole at a slight angle through the hands as shown in (B). Stay towards the back of the hands so you will have enough wood to round the front. *Note: the bit and hand placement is shown in the right hand photo as a reference only. Please use caution and care by mounting the block into a suitable work holder.*

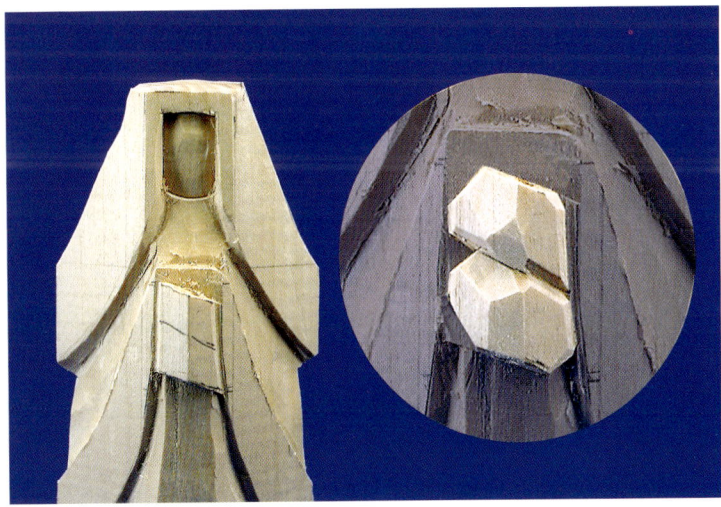

9. Trim the hand area using a knife so that it appears like the inset on the right hand photo.

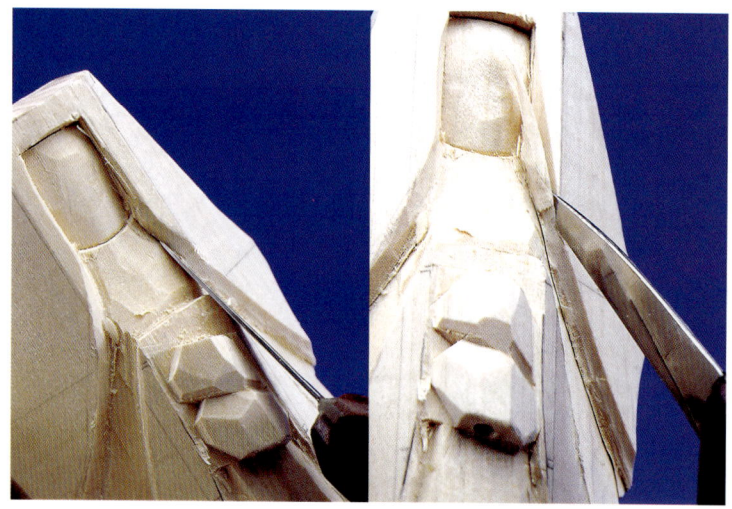

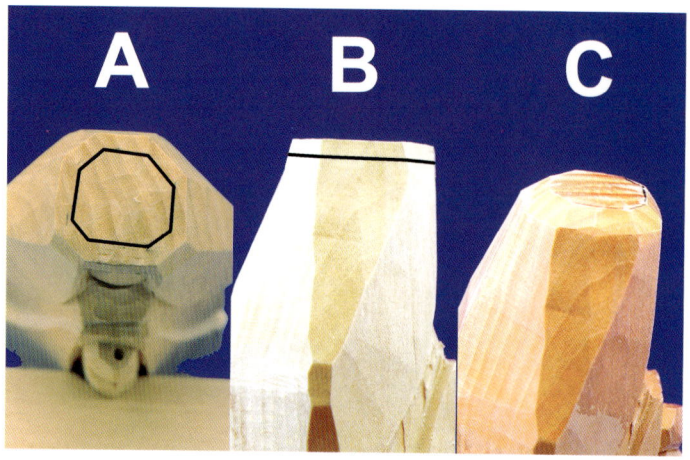

10. Next we will begin cleaning up the cuts. Using the knife, make a cut along the head covering on the left. Next, make a cut to remove the small sliver of wood as shown in the photo on the right. *Note: Only make these cuts on the bottom sides of the shawl and the robe to enhance the shadow effect.*

12. Mark a line 1/8 inch along the top of the head covering as shown in (A). Mark a line 1/8 inch along the top side of the head covering as shown in (B). Use the knife and remove this wedge along the edge as shown in (C).

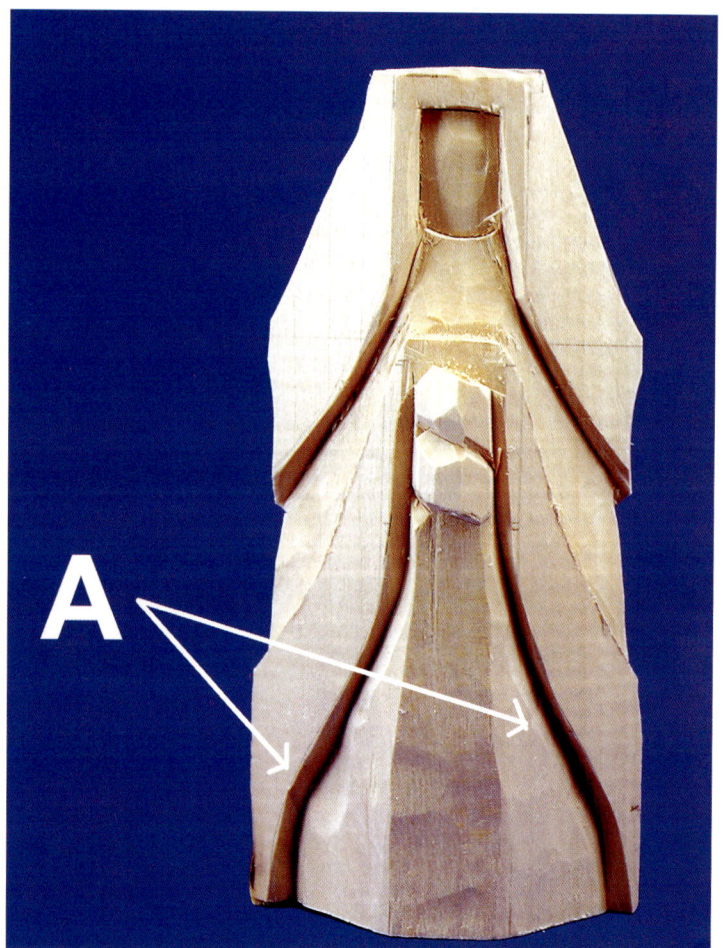

13. Using a worn out piece of 220 to 320 grit sandpaper, rub down the carving. Take care not to sand too hard and remove the details. You want the carving to look hand worn. Cut a 5-1/4 inch, 3/16 inch dowel and insert it into the hands. You may want to take the knife and texture the rod to remove the roundness. Progress for the front and right side of the shepherd.

11. Clean up the base where the cloak covers the robe. Notice the nice shadow lines as indicated by (A). Refer to Steps 74 and 75 in Chapter One -- Mary.

14. Progress for the back and left side of the shepherd.

Chapter Five
Angel

The angel is a variation on the other pieces you have carved so far. The angel consists of two pieces, the body and the wings. We want the angel to be tall and thin. To obtain this look, we will need a 1-1/2 inch by 1-1/2 inch by 8 inch block of Basswood. In addition, you will need a 3 inch by 5-3/4 inch by 3/8 inch piece of Basswood for the wings and 2-inches of 3/16 inch dowel rod. Cut out the wings using the pattern supplied.

You will follow the same general guidelines to carve the angel. The first step is to mark in the shoulder line.

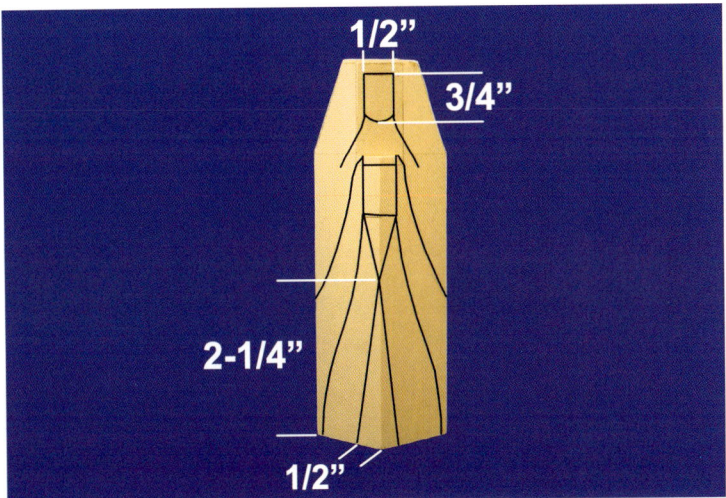

3. Refer back to Chapter One -- Mary, Steps 2-20, for removing the wedges that form the top of the carving. Transfer the dimensions shown to the block.

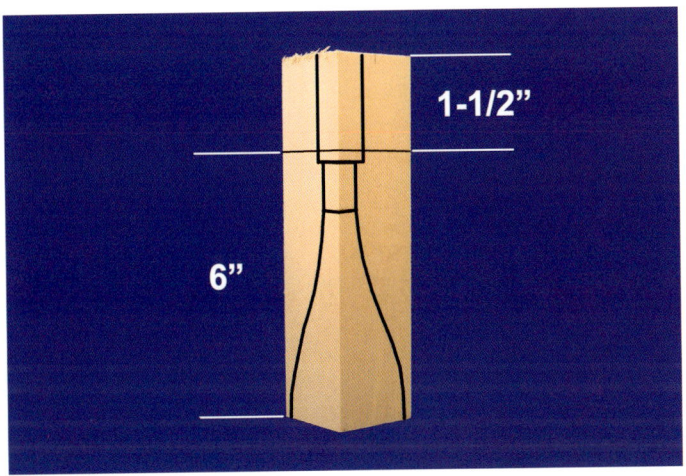

1. Using a ruler, mark a line 1-1/2-inches on the side of the block. Continue this line around the block.

4. Refer back to the steps for Chapter One -- Mary, Steps 21-26, 29-80 to block in the body of the angel. The front and right sides are shown.

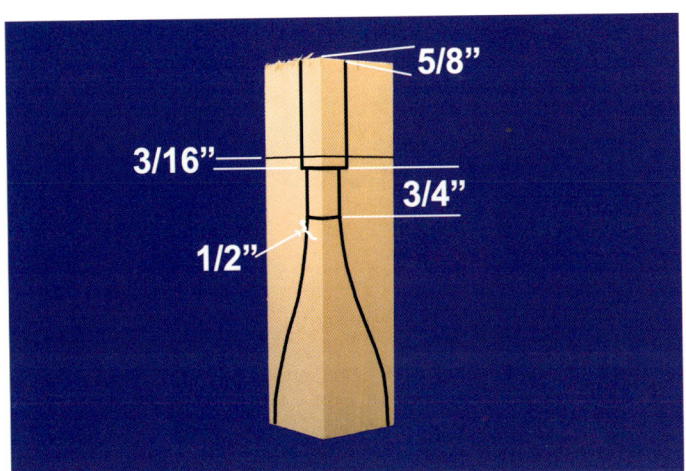

2. Lay out the block using the dimensions.

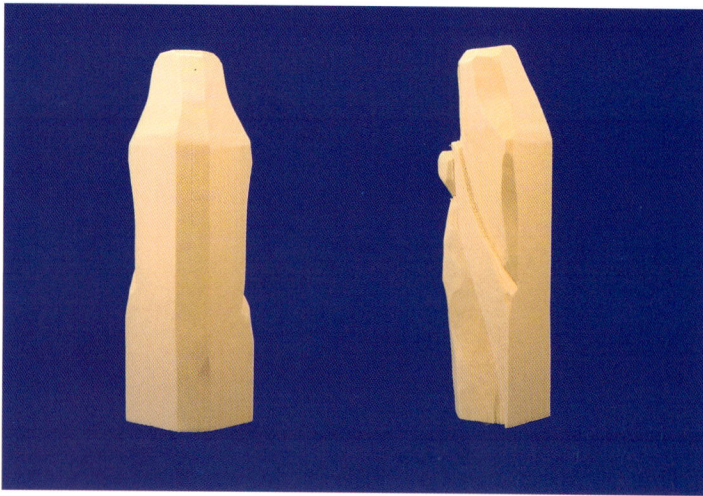

5. The Angel body, the back, and left sides are shown.

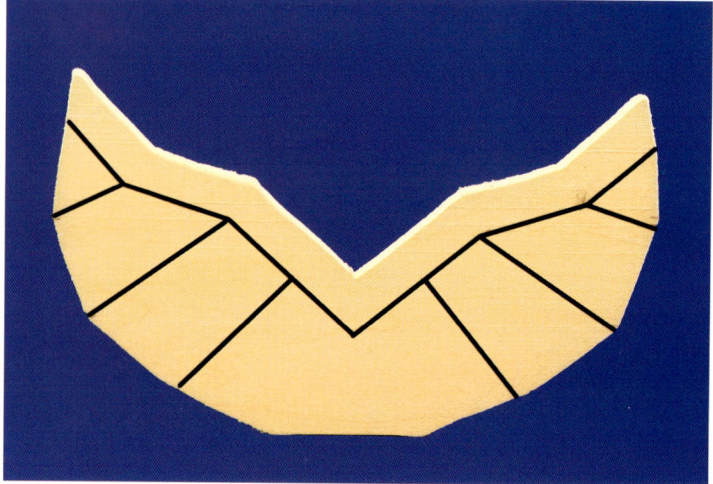

6. Using the pattern template supplied, transfer the lines to the wings.

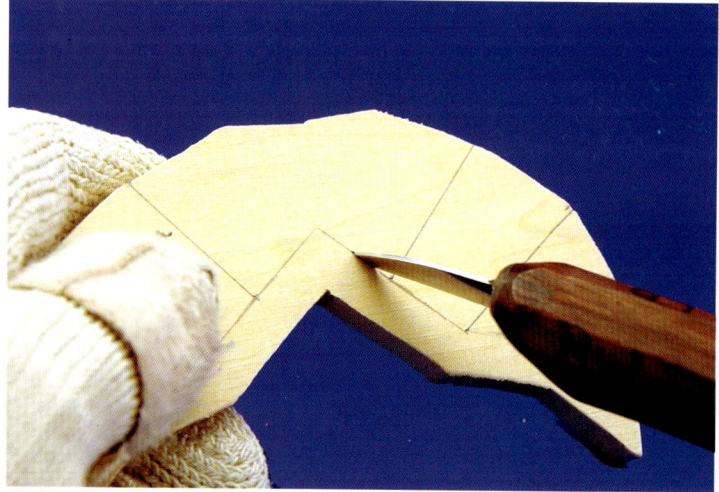

7. Using a knife, start about 3/8 inch from the intersection and cut along the top of the wings as shown in the photo. This cut should be approximately 1/8 inch deep.

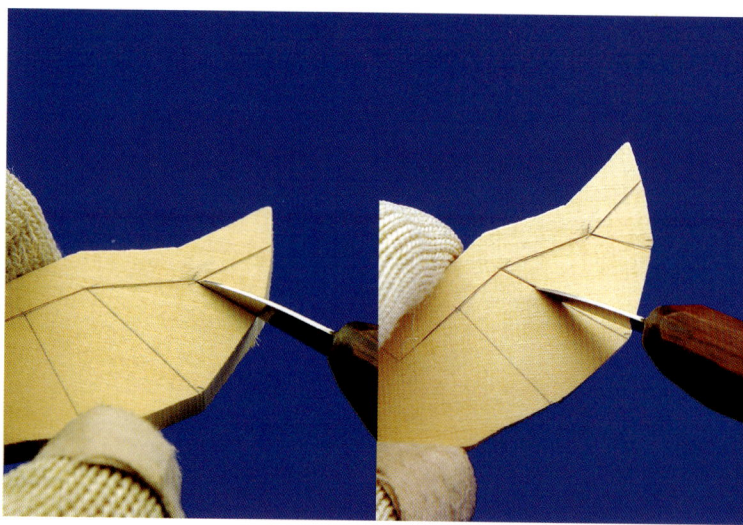

8. Using the knife, make a stop cut along the lines that go from the top of the wing to the edges as shown in the photo.

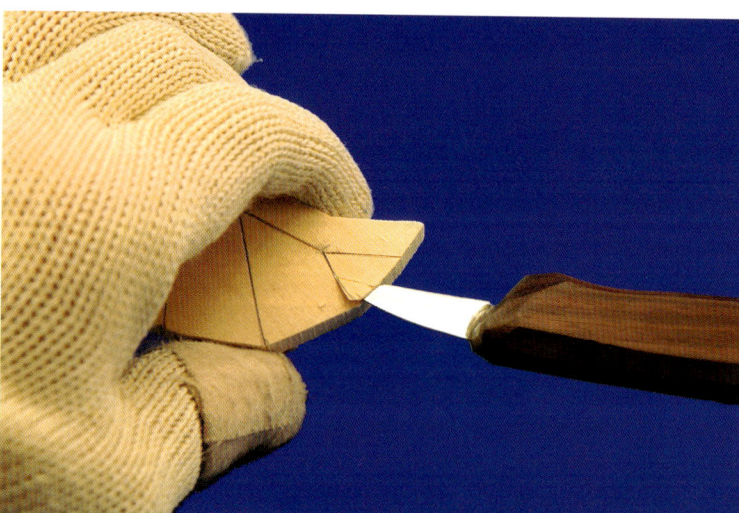

9. Remove the wedge-shaped piece of the wing as shown in the photo. Do this for the rest of the wing. Note: the wings taper from the thick part (bottom) to the thin (top) of the wing.

10. Your wings should like this. Remember to leave a flat space in the middle of the base of the wings so they can be attached the wings to the body of the angel.

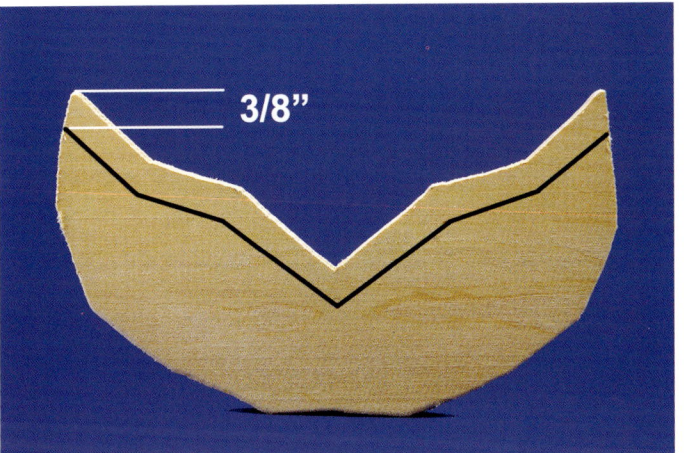

11. To remove the blocky look, we will remove the square edges of the wing. Mark in a line 3/8 inch along the back side of the wings. The front of the wings will have a shorter taper than the back side. Mark a 3/16 inch line on the front side of the wings.

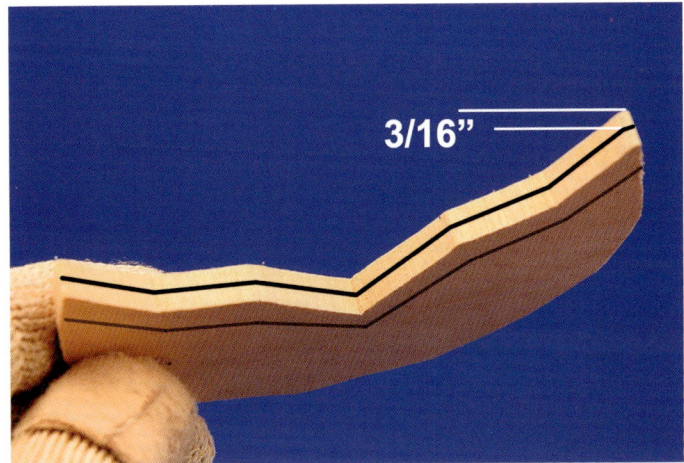

12. Draw a line down the middle of the wings on the top. The middle should be around 3/16 inch in from either side.

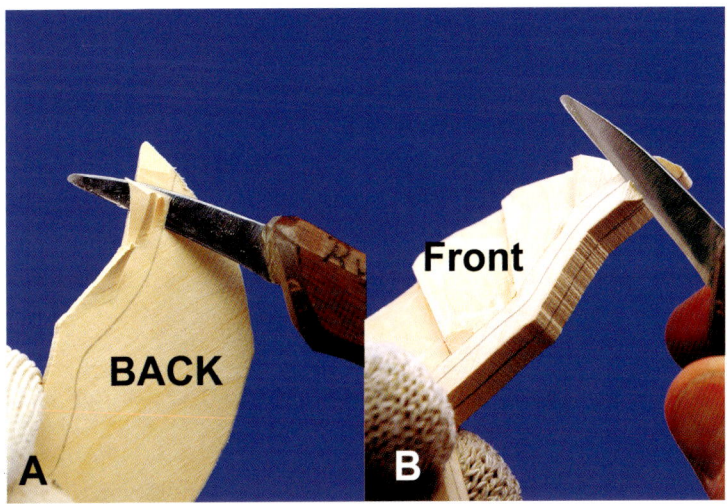

13. Using the knife, remove a wedge along the back as shown in the right-hand photo. This wedge will be longer on the back than on the top. Use the knife to remove a wedge shape piece of wood along the front of the wing as shown in the left-hand photo.

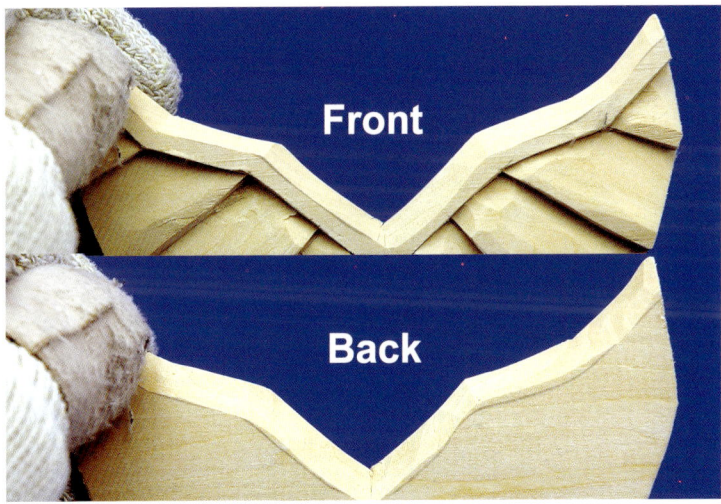

14. Progress so far. Your wings should look like the photo.

The wings are attached to the body using 3/16 inch dowels. Drill two 3-16 inch holes in the center of the wings approximately 1/2 inch apart, starting 1/4 inch from the bottom of the wing. The next step is to mount the wings. This will require you to hold the wings on the back while looking at the front to ensure that the wings are balanced side-to-side and not up too high.

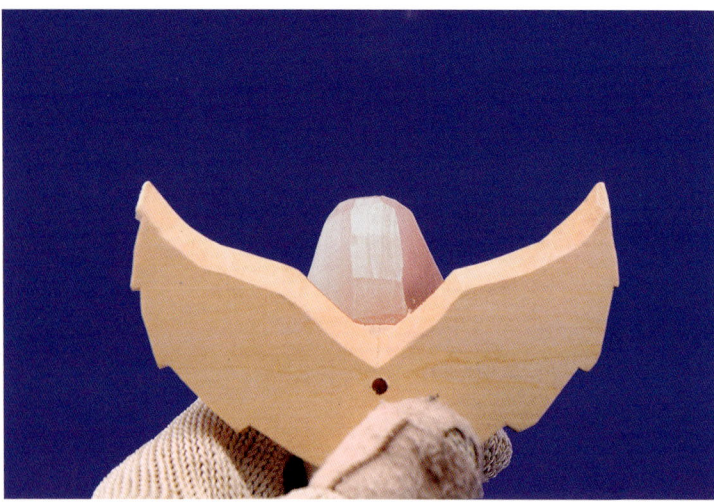

15. When you are satisfied with the placement, mark the center of the top hole with a pencil. Drill a 3/16 inch hole 5/8 inch deep into the back of the angel at the mark. Cut a 1 inch length of 3/16 inch dowel and place it in the hole in the back of the angel. Slide the wings over the dowel.

Completed angel, front and right sides. Using a worn out piece of 220 to 320 grit sandpaper, rub down the carving. Take care not to sand too hard and remove the details. You want the carving to look hand worn.

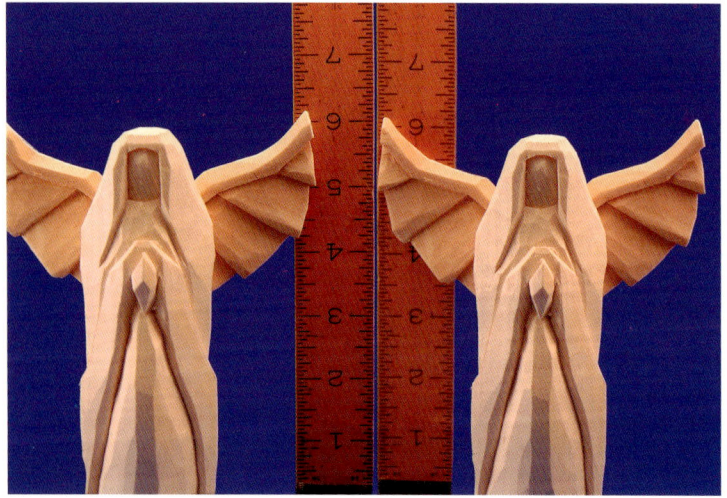

16. Use a ruler to ensure that the tips of the wings are the same height for balance. When you are satisfied with the placement, mark the center of the bottom hole with a pencil. Remove the wings and then drill a 3/16 inch hole, 5/8 inch deep into the back of the angel at the mark. Cut a 1 inch length of 3/16 inch dowel and place it in the hole in the back of the angel. Slide the wings over the dowels for final assembly. Use a knife or the #3 gouge and cut the dowels to be flush with the back of the wings.

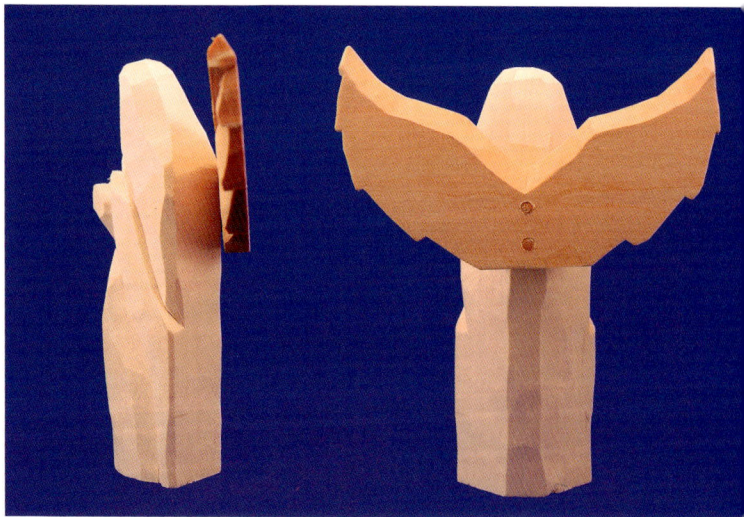

18. Completed angel back and left sides.

Chapter Six
Kneeling King Melchior and Chest of Gold

Melchior was the Sultan of Arabia. He was the oldest of the Magi and was a small and gentle man. His gift to the holy family was gold, which was much used by the Hebrews for the Temple fixtures and was very plentiful in the time of David and Solomon. In carving King Melchior, we will have him kneeling, and is similar to carving Joseph; however, we will carve Melchior with a different headpiece. For this king, you will need a 2 inch by 2 inch by 6 inch block of Basswood. You will notice that this is 1/4 inch longer that Joseph. The extra 1/4 inch will be used for a crown. In addition, you will need a 1-1/4 inch by 1-1/4 inch by 1-1/2 inch long piece of Basswood for the chest (the grain runs the 1-1/2 inch length).

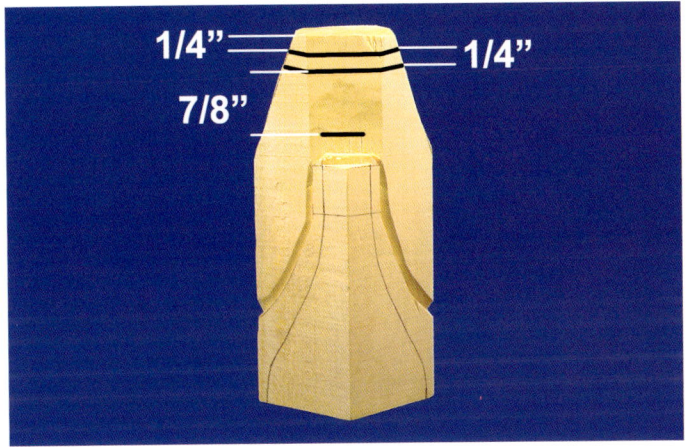

1. Refer back to the section on carving Joseph and carve your block to look like the photo shown. Mark a line 1/4 inch below the top and another line 1/4 inch below the first. These two lines will provide guides to carving the crown. Now, place a mark 7/8 inch below the bottom mark to indicate the base of the face.

2. Extend the two lines all the way around the carving.

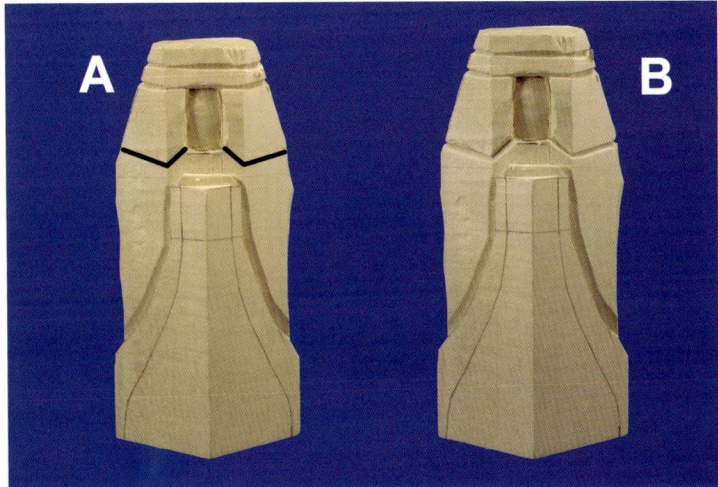

3. Place a mark 1 inch below the bottom line of the crown as shown in (A). Extend this line all the way around the carving. This will represent the head covering that was worn under the crown. Take the V-tool and remove the line around the base of the head covering as shown in (B).

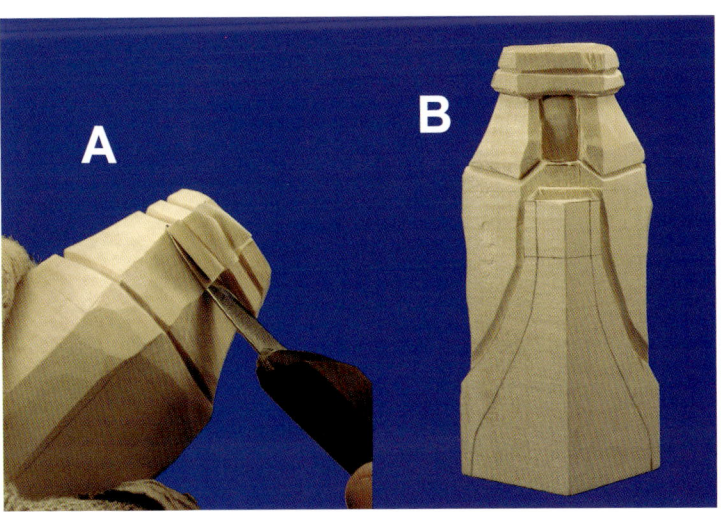

4. Using the knife, remove the wood of the head covering and cut up towards the crown. Take care not to cut off the crown as you make these cuts. If you do, glue it back on and continue.

5. King Melchior, progress so far, front and right sides.

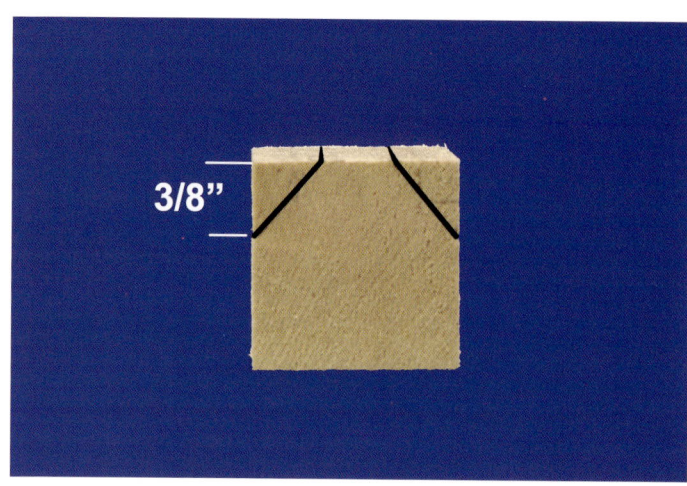

8. Mark lines 3/8 inch down on both sides of the block and connect the line from the top to the side as shown.

6. King Melchior, progress so far, back and left sides.

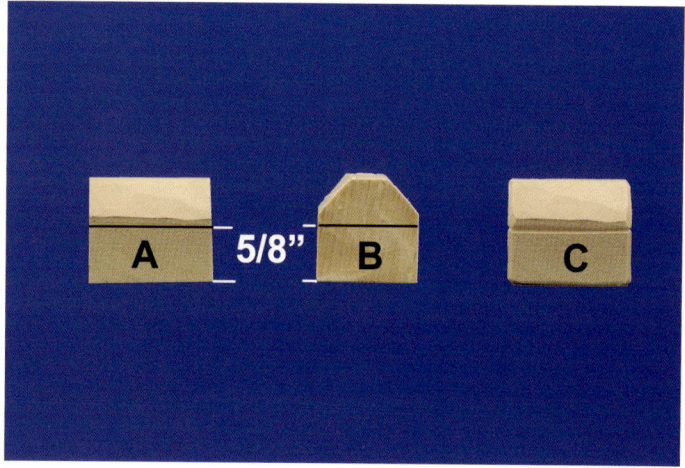

9. Using a knife, remove this wedge on both sides of the block, as can be seen in the photos. Mark a line 5/8 inch from the bottom of the block as shown in (A) and (B). Use the V tool and remove this line as shown in (C). This gives the impression of the lid for the chest.

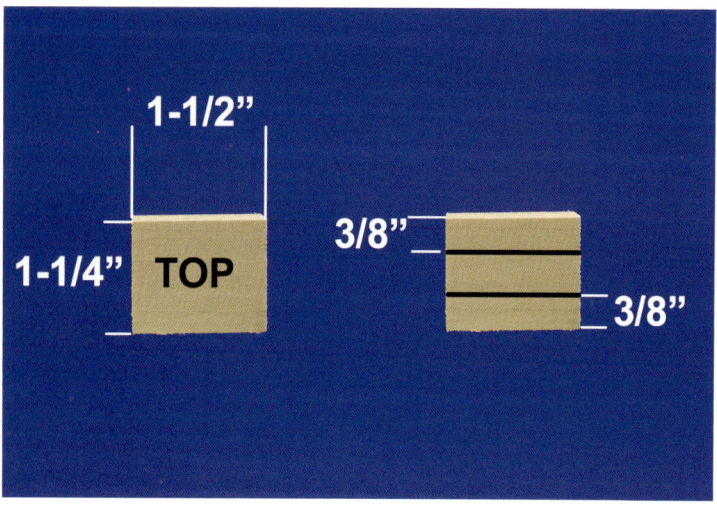

7. Take the 1-1/4 inch by 1-1/2 inch by 1-1/2 inch block and mark a line 3/8 inch on both sides of the top as shown in the photo on the right.

10. King Melchoir and the chest. Using a worn out piece of 220 to 320 grit sandpaper, rub down the carving. Take care not to sand too hard and remove the details. You want the carving to look hand worn.

Chapter Seven
Standing King Gaspar

King Gaspar was Emperor of the Orient and ruled over all Oriental lands at the time of Jesus' birth. His gift to the baby Jesus was Frankincense. It is an exceedingly aromatic resin distilled from trees found in Arabia. Frankincense was considered to be a priceless gift for Kings, and symbolized prayer. The standing kings are carved similar to the Shepherd; however, they will have a different headpiece, hands, and crowns. Kings Gaspar and Baltazar are carrying gifts that are similar in shape and size. You will need a 2 inch by 2 inch by 6-3/4 or 7 inch block of Basswood for each king. Varying the size will keep the kings from looking too similar.

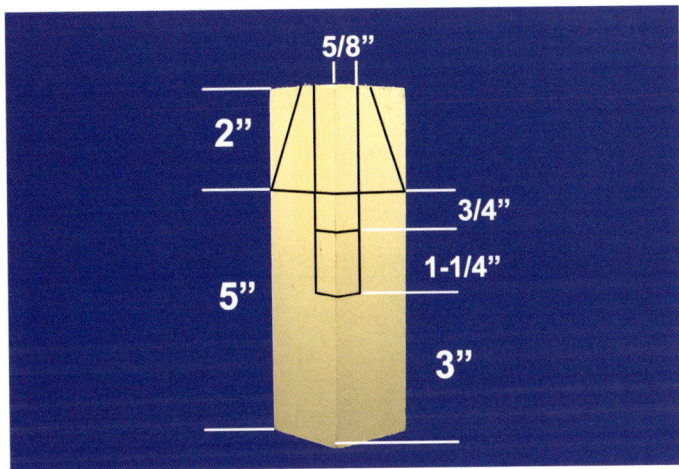

1. Lay out the block as shown in the photo. The shoulder line is the standard 2 inch line that goes all the way around the block. The top of the gift is 3/4 inch below the shoulder line, and the area for the gift is 1-1/4 inch in length.

2. Carve the king so that it looks like the photo. Refer to the chapter on carving the Shepherd. Using the template, mark in the top and bottom of the robe.

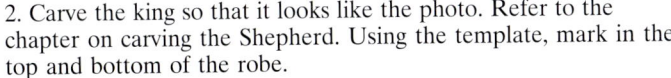

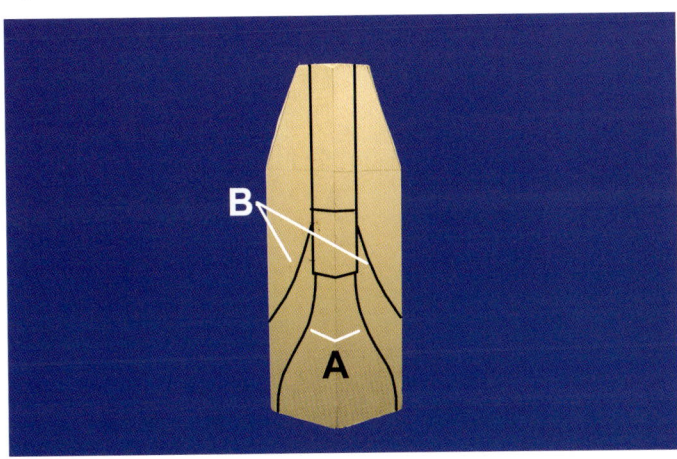

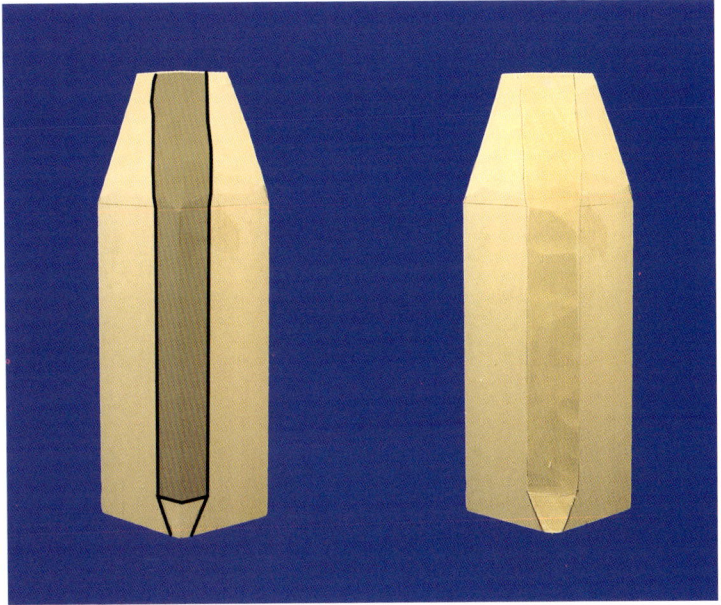

3. Remove the wedge along the back as shown in the photo.

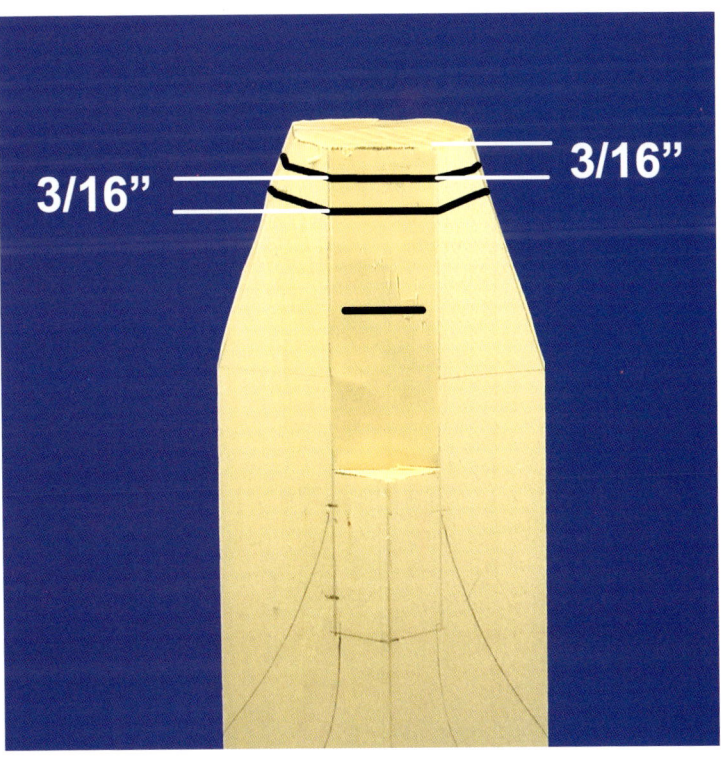

4. The crown will be two-tiered. Mark a line 3/16 inch down from the top and another line 3/16 inch below the previous line.

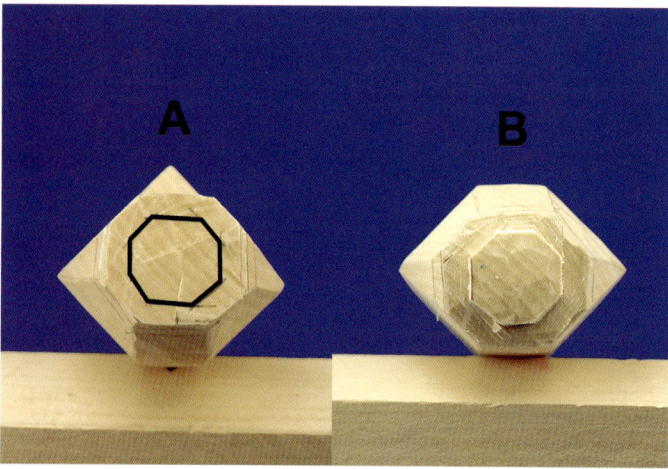

5. Mark a line 3/16 inch in all around the top of the crown as shown in the photo shown. Using a knife, make a stop cut along the lines on the side and remove the wood from the top. Your crown should look similar to (B).

6. Mark a line 1 inch below the bottom of the crown. Continue this line around the carving. This line will rise towards the back so that head will appear to be bowing.

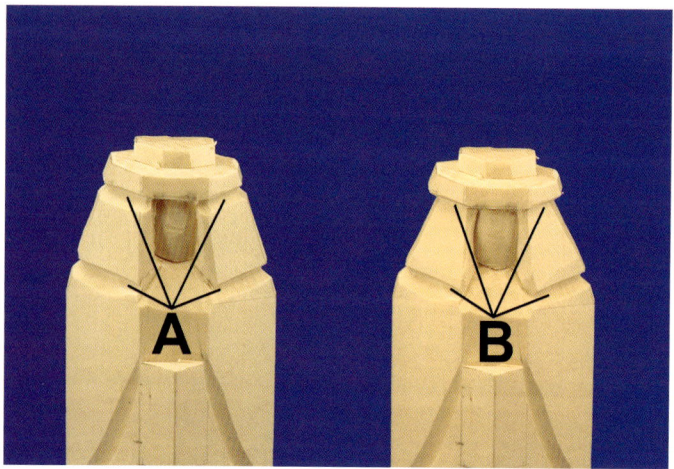

7. Using a V-tool and knife, remove the wood around the headpiece and the crown as shown in (A). Using a knife, taper the sides of the headpiece so that it tucks under the crown as shown in (B). Take care not to cut off the crown.

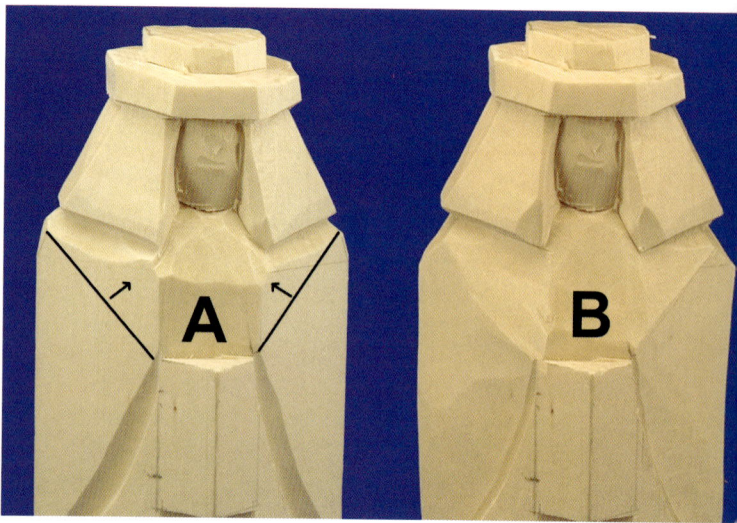

8. Draw a line from the ends of the hand area to the shoulder line as shown in (A). Using a knife, remove the wood as shown in (B). This should taper from the hands to the face.

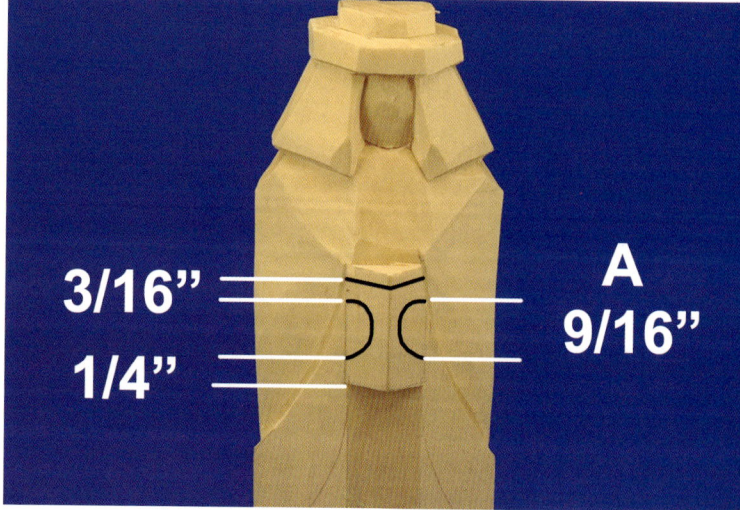

9. Mark a line 1/4 inch above the base of the hand/gifts in (A). Mark another line 9/16 inch above the previous mark. Mark a line 3/16 inch above the top of the hands. Draw in the semi-circles to represent the hands on both sides of the gift.

10. Using the #7-5/8 inch gouge, make a cut outline and set in the hands.

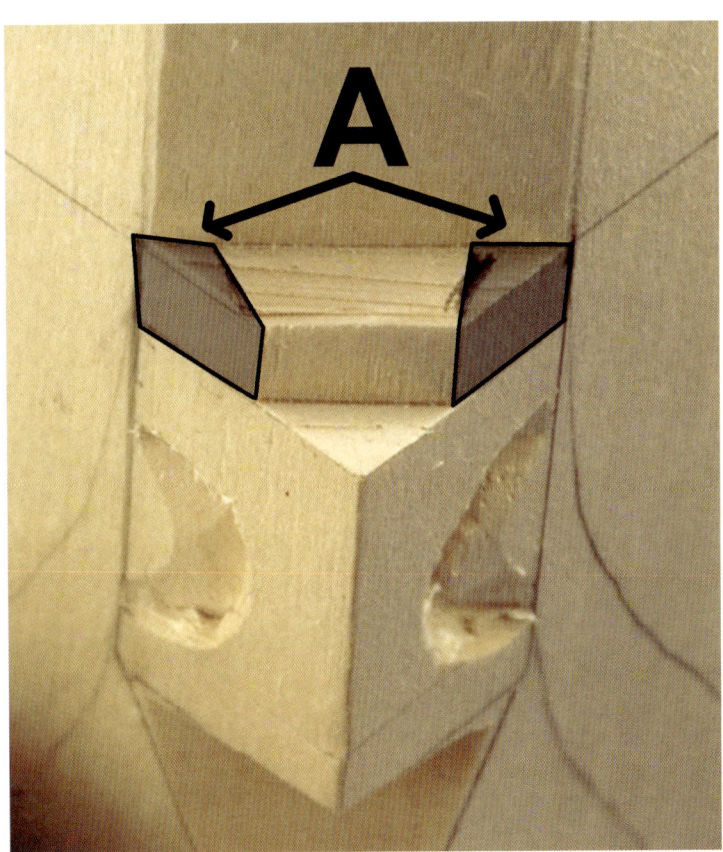

12. We will carve this king holding a jar, which will represent the container for the frankincense. First we will block in the lid as shown in (A). Use the knife to remove the two small wedge shaped areas (shaded).

11. King Gaspar, progress so far.

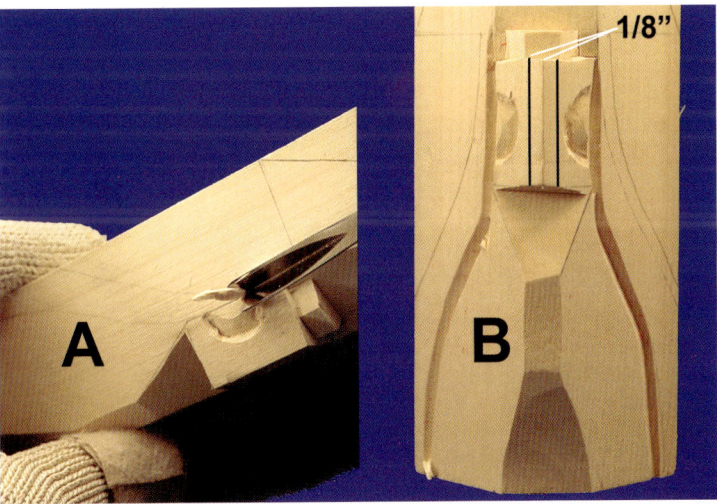

13. Take the V-tool and make a cut along side the robe area as shown in (A). Mark a line 1/8 inch on both sides of the front of the block as shown in (B). Use the knife to remove the wood between these marks. This will remove the sharp edge and make the jar look octagonal in shape.

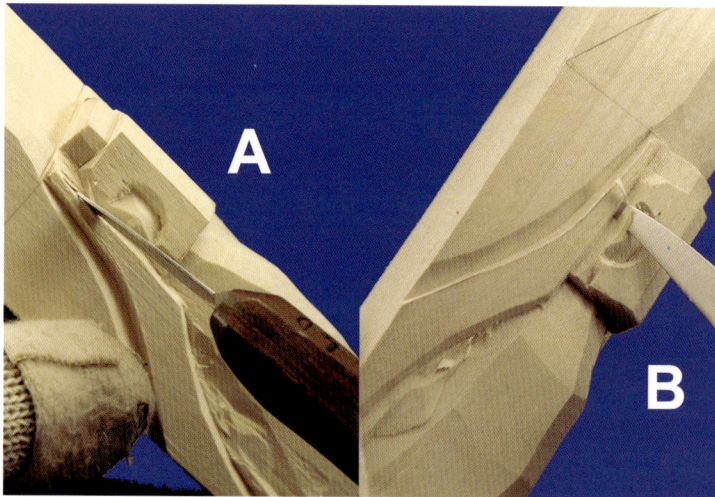

14. We need to make the hands appear to be coming out from under the robe. To do this, make a cut perpendicular to the hand area as shown in (A). Next make a cut along side the hand area to remove the wedge as shown in (B).

16. Completed King Gaspar, front and right sides.

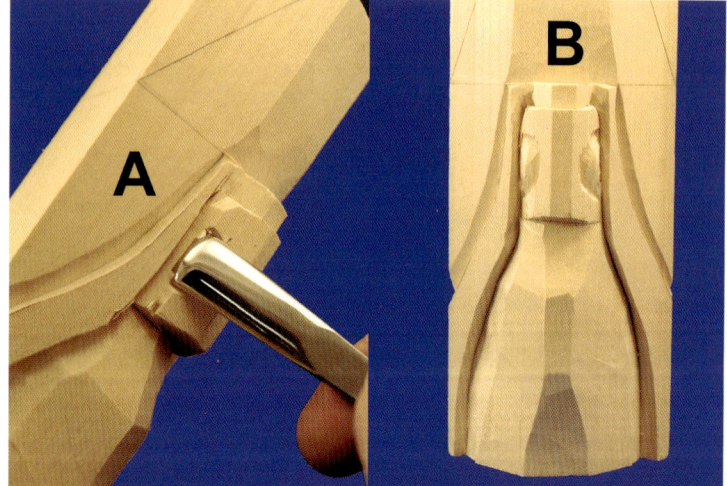

15. The last cuts should have removed some of the roundness of the hands where they enters under the robe. To clean up the hand area and to deepen the hands, take the #7-5/8 gouge and re-cut the hands as shown in (B).

Go over the rest of the carving and remove any fuzzy cuts. Take a piece of worn out 220-330 grit sandpaper and lightly sand the completed carving. This will provide a hand rubbed look when we put on the final finish.

17. Completed King Gaspar, back and left sides.

Chapter Eight
Standing King Baltazar

Baltazar was a Nubian King and the ruler of Ethiopia. His gift to baby Jesus was myrrh, an aromatic resin that comes from the bark of thorny African trees symbolized suffering. The standing kings are carved similar to the Shepherd; however, they will have a different headpiece and crowns. The gifts they carry are similar in shape and size. You will need a 2 inch by 2 inch by 6-3/4 or 7 inch block of Basswood for each king. If you used a 6-3/4 inch block for King Gaspar, use a 7 inch block for this king. This will keep the kings from looking too similar.

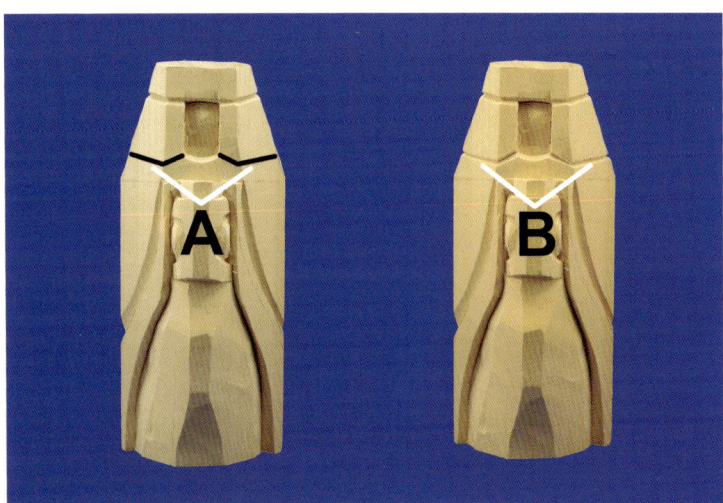

3. Referring to Chapter 4, go ahead and cut in the face of the king. Draw a line from the edge of the 1 inch line to the bottom corner of the face as shown in (A). Take the V-tool and remove the line around the base of the crown and the bottom of the headpiece as shown in (B).

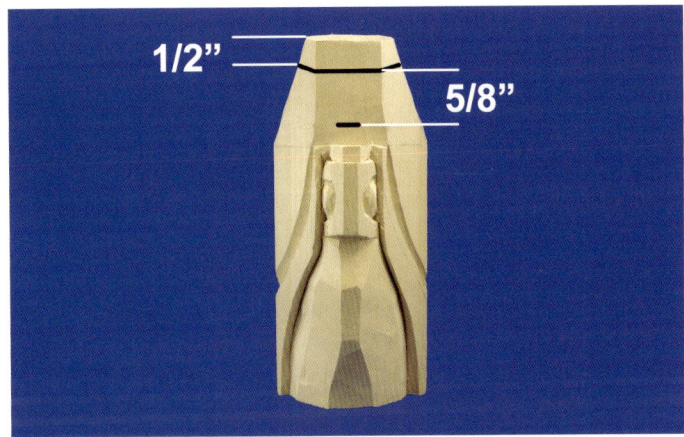

1. Lay out the block in the same manner as King Gaspar, step one. The shoulder line is the standard 2 inch line that goes all the way around the block. The top of the gift is 3/4 inch below the shoulder line, and the area for the gift is 1-1/4 inch in length.

Referring to chapters 4 and 7, carve the king so that it looks like the photo. Mark a line 1/2 inch below the top of the block all the way around. This will be the bottom of the crown. Mark another line 5/8 inch below the previous line. This will mark the bottom of the face.

2. Draw a line 1 inch below the base of the crown. Transfer this line all the way around the carving.

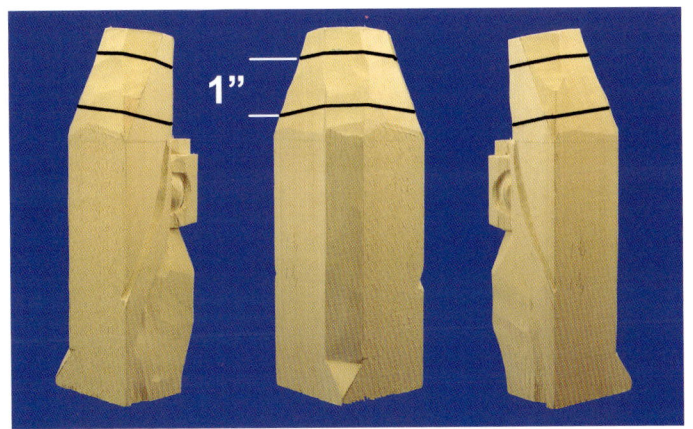

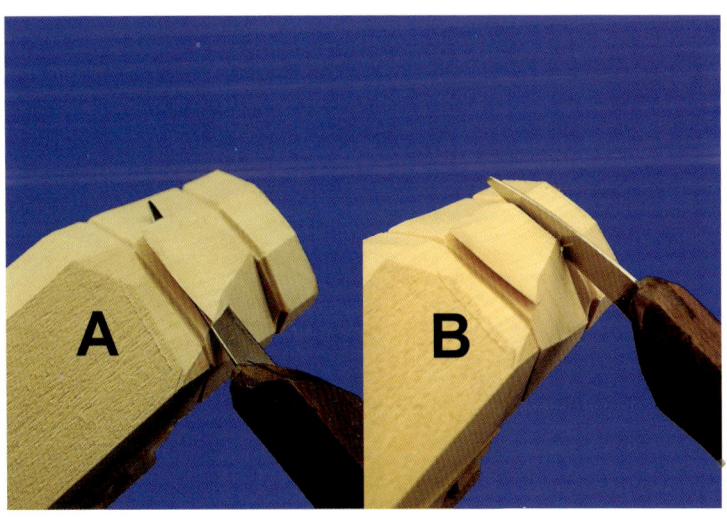

4. Using the knife, start tapering the headpiece to fit under the crown in (A). Make a stop cut as shown in (B) to remove the risk of cutting or breaking off the crown.

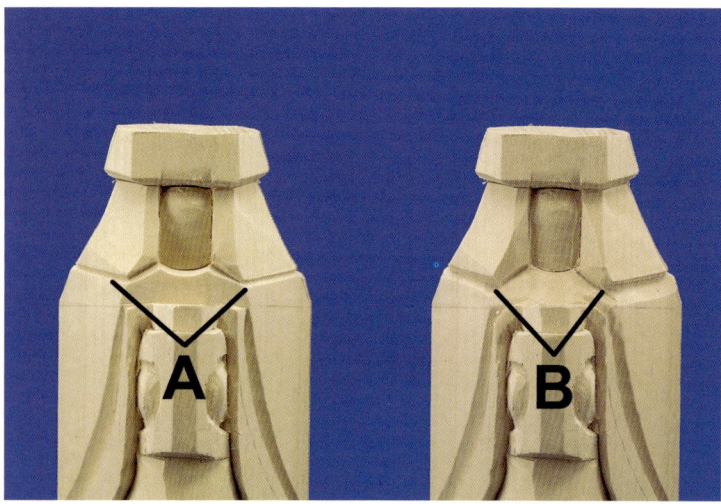

5. Taper the ends of the headpiece as indicated in (A). Note the smooth transition from the corner to the edge of the headpiece as shown in (B).

7. Completed King Baltazar, front and right sides.

6. The crown will be a single-tier crown and will taper from the top of the crown to to the top of the head. Using the knife, taper the crown.

8. Completed King Baltazar, back and left sides. Go over the rest of the carving and remove any fuzzy cuts. Take a piece of worn out 220-330 grit sandpaper and lightly sand the complete carving.

Chapter Nine
Camel

The camel is a companion piece to go with the three kings. You may want to carve one or more to include with your nativity set. The patterns supplied provide a standing and a sitting camel. You may wish to interchange the backs of the camels during layout if you would rather have a Dromedary (single hump) camel. Note of interest: the Bactrian camels are often confused with Dromedary camels, who only have one hump and typically live in hot, desert climates. In contrast, Bactrian camels have two humps and are native to the cold mountain and high desert climates of Central Asia.

You will need a piece of 1-1/2 inch thick Basswood, 4-inches tall and 6-1/2 inches in width. Note, the grain runs vertical to provide the strength for the fragile pieces, i.e. neck and ears. The camel will be carved in flat plane style with large flat facets. We will only remove enough wood to provide a resemblance to the camel. If you opt for the standing camel, make sure it sits flat on the bottom so it doesn't tip over. *Note: I have found in the seminars that I have taught, that students have a hard time not rounding the animals. Resist the urge to round!*

Using the pattern supplied, trace and cut out the camel blank.

1. Transfer the measurements above to the camel blank. Draw a line from the back side of the ears to where the camel's chin transitions to the neck as shown by (A). Draw a line 1/2 inch from the edge from the neck (A) to the tail section. Mark a line 2-1/4 inch from back (D) and make another mark 1/8 inch past that mark approximately 3/8 inch above and 2-1/4 inch mark. Draw a line tapering from the base to this point. Continue the line back towards the middle of the back as shown in (C). This line will represent the back legs that are folded under the camel. Mark a line 2-1/4 inch from the front in (E). Draw a line vertically about 1/2 inch and then draw another line approximately 1/2 long towards the neck as shown in the photo.

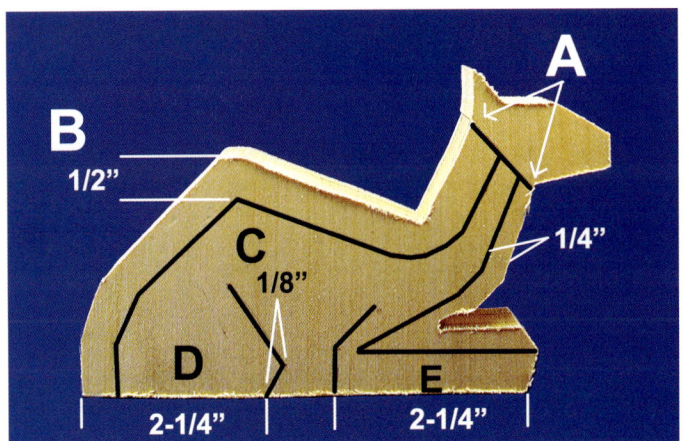

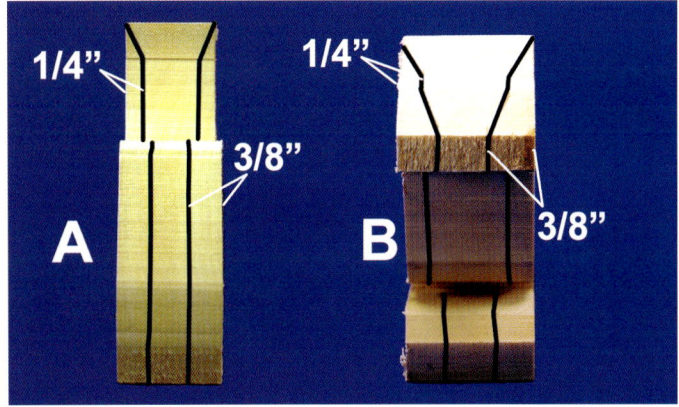

2. Draw a line 3/8 inch in on both sides of the camel blank. Flare the line to the tips of the ears in (A). On the front side, taper the lines in to the face 1/4 inch (B) and continue the line to the nose.

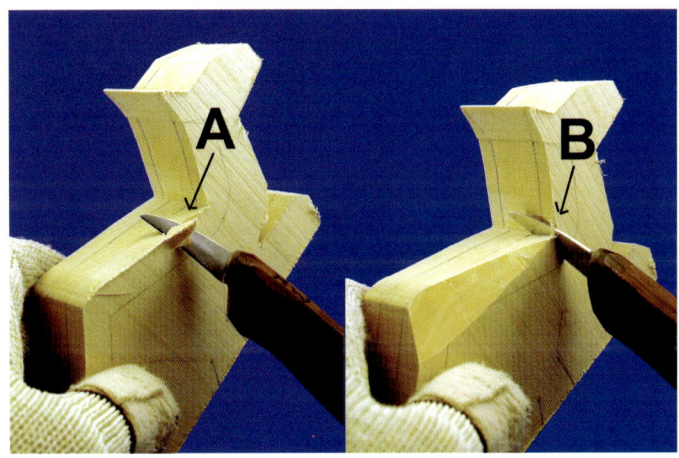

3. Using the knife, remove the wedge as shown in (A). Since the grain is running vertically, you will have to watch how you make the cuts. Make a stop cut at the base of the neck as shown in (B).

4. Make a stop cut at the base of the ears as shown in (A). Remove the wedge of wood as shown in (B) so that in the following steps you don't inadvertently cut off the ear.

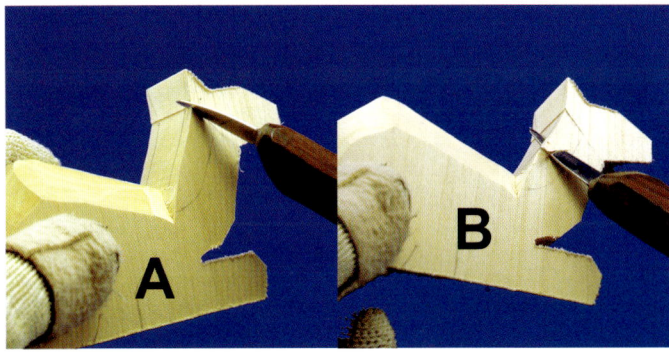

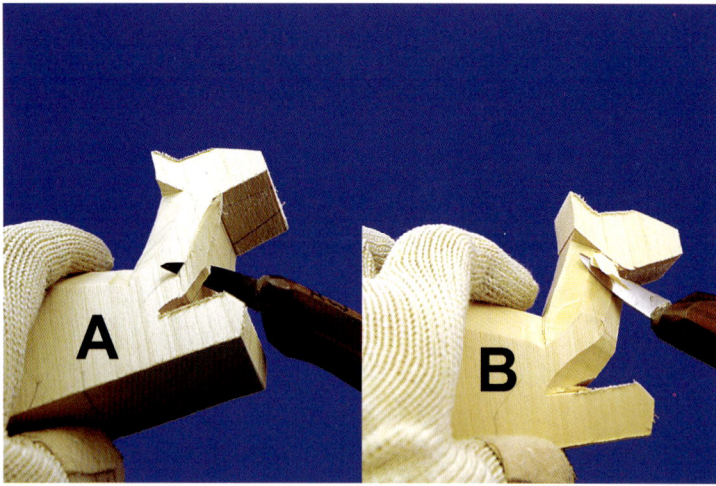

5. Taper the side of the neck into the base of the head as shown in (A). Remove the front edge as shown in (B).

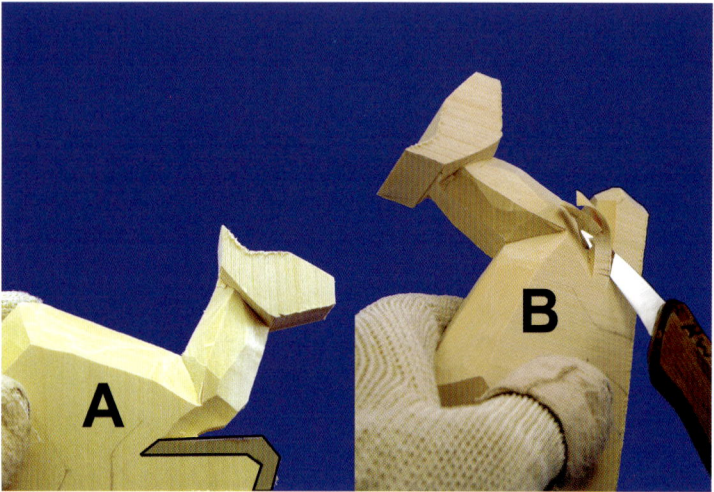

6. Progress so far is shown in (A). Mark a line 1/4 inch from the top and front edges as shown by the shadowed area. Take the knife and remove this area as shown in (B).

7. Taper the sides of the face as shown in (A). Progress so far in (B).

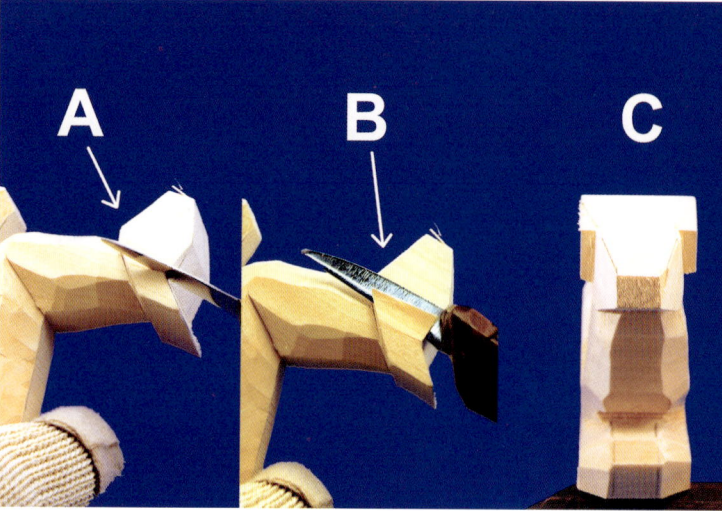

8. Make a stop cut at the base of the ears as shown in (A). Remove wood from the front of the ear as shown in (B). Progress so far is shown in (C).

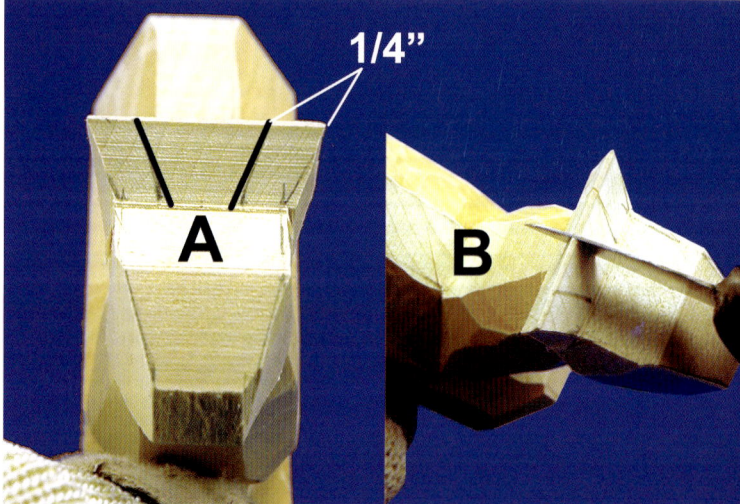

9. Mark a line 1/4 inch parallel to the outside edge as shown in (A). Starting in the middle, make *small* cuts and remove the wood between the ears of the camel as shown in (B). Take care to not break or cut off the ears.

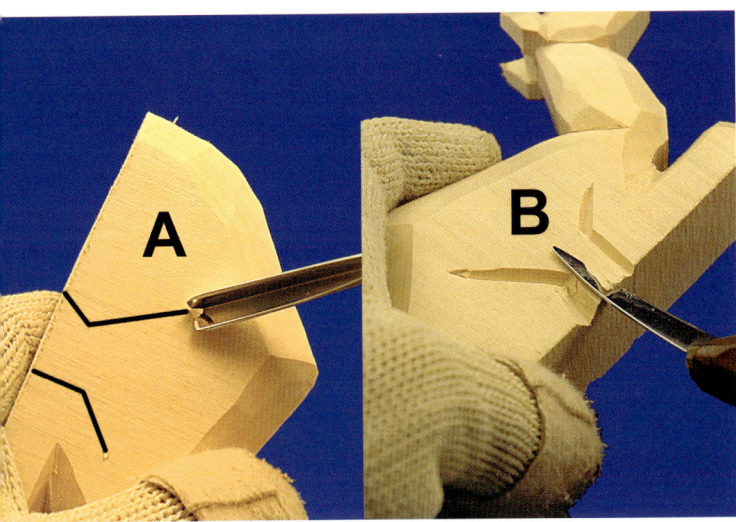

10. Take the V-tool and remove the lines as shown in (A). Take the knife and remove the wood between the front and back legs as shown in (B). Taper these cuts so that the belly appears to go under the camel.

11. Taper the sides of the camel slightly. The side of your camel will be straight since this is the way it started. Go over the carving and remove any saw marks or other blemishes.

12. Progress of the camel so far. Take a piece of worn out 220-320 grit paper and gently sand the carving for the hand rubbed look. Go over the rest of the carving and remove any fuzzy cuts.
Take a piece of worn out 220-330 grit sandpaper and lightly sand the completed carving.

Chapter Ten
Ox

Even though the ox and donkey were not specifically mentioned in the Christmas accounts of the gospels, no nativity scene would be complete without them. Throughout the ages, the ox and donkey have been added to the manger scene because of the reference in scripture about the animals being more faithful than God's people. "An ox knows its owner, and an ass, its master's manger, But Israel does not know, my people do not understand" Isaiah 1:3. The ox and donkey are mentioned as part of the manger scene in apocryphal writings about Christ's life (writings which the Church did not accept as inspired and belonging in the Bible.) They were present in nativity representations as early as the fourth century.

For the ox, you will need a piece of 1-1/2 inch thick Basswood, 2-1/2 inches tall and 5-1/2 inches wide. Note, the grain runs vertically to provide the strength for the fragile pieces, i.e. horns and ears. The ox will be carved in flat plane style with large, flat facets. We will only remove enough wood to provide a resemblance to the ox. Note: Resist the urge to round! Using the pattern supplied, trace and cut out the ox blank.

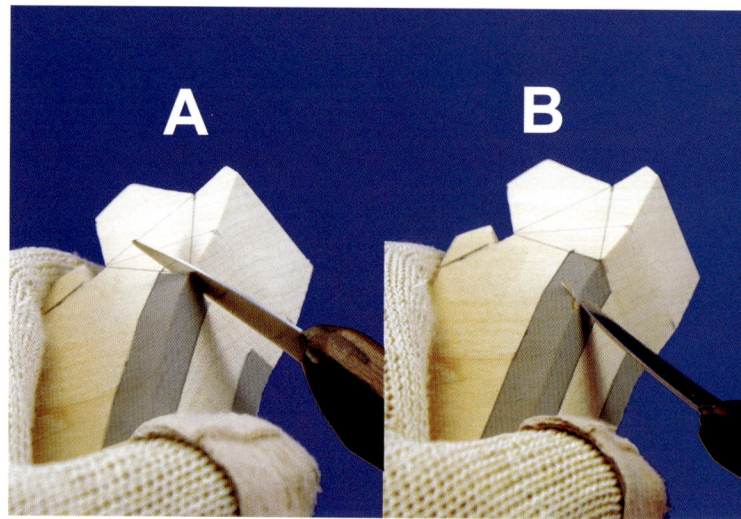

2. Make a stop cut on the back side of the ears as shown in (A). Remove the small wedge behind the ear. This will help prevent removing the ear accidentally as you make the cuts on the neck. Remove the wood along the back of the hind quarters (shaded area) as shown in (B).

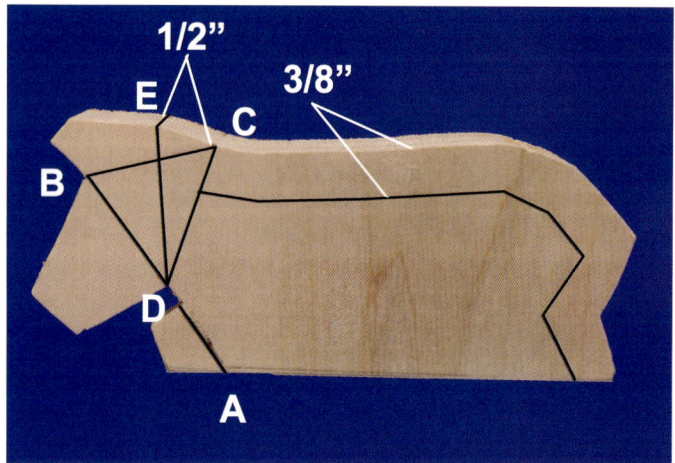

1. Transfer the measurements above to the ox blank. Draw a line from the bottom to the front of the legs (A) to (D). Continue this line from (D) to (B). Draw a line from (B) to (C) (where the base of the head transitions to the back). Continue the line to (D). Note: the distance from (C) to (E) is 1/2 inch. Draw a line from (D) to (E). Draw a line 3/8 inch from the edge from the neck (A) to the tail section. Mark these lines on both sides.

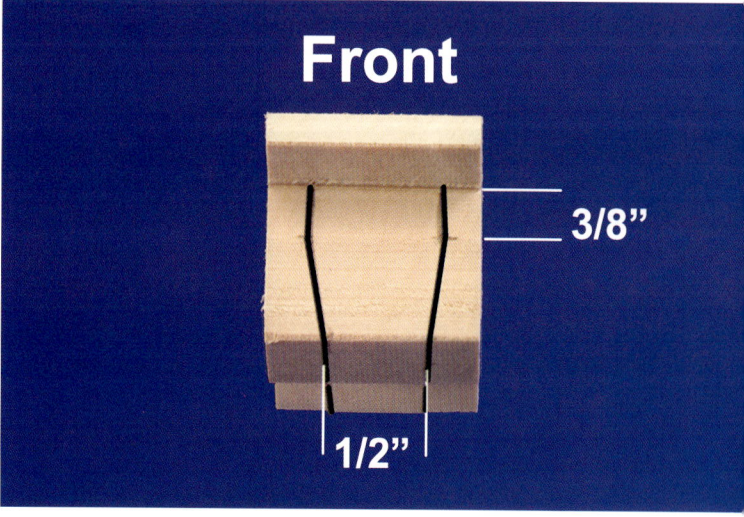

3. Transfer the measures from the photo to your blank. The brow of the ox is 3/8 inch from the base of the horns and approximately 1/4 inch in from the sides. The face tapers to 1/2 inch at the front.

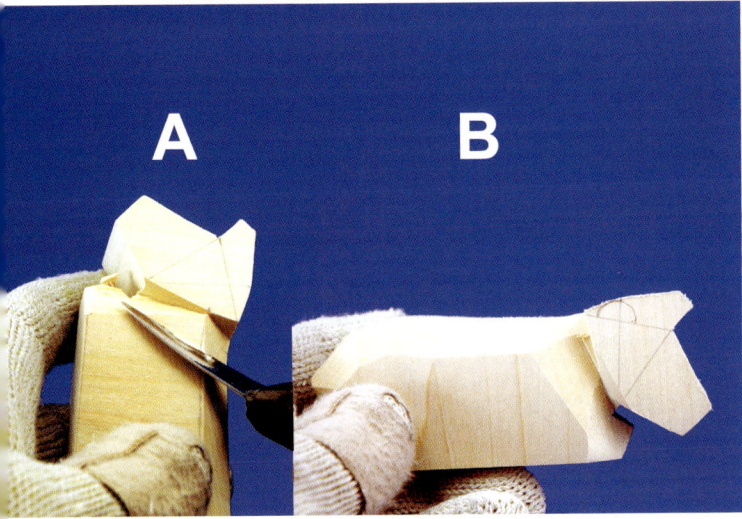

4. Make a stop along the line (C) to (D) drawn in step 1. Remove the wedge of wood as shown in (B). This will taper the neck to the head.

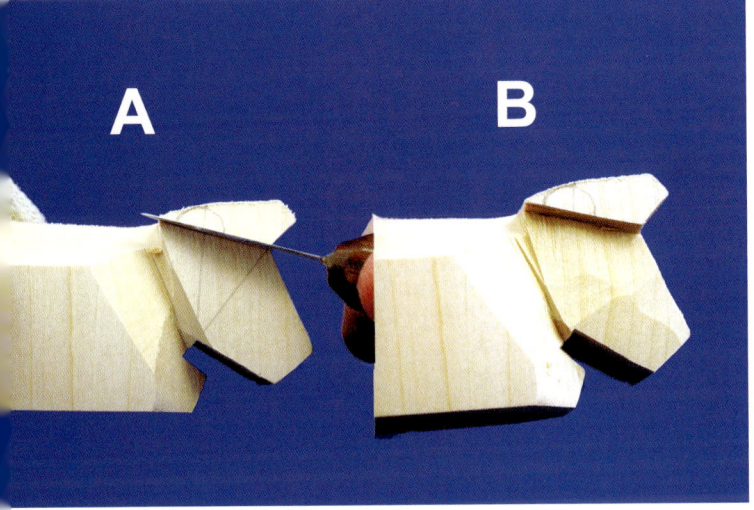

5. Make a stop cut along the (B) to (C) line as drawn in step 1. Remove the wedge of wood below the horns/ears as shown in (B). This will taper the head to the horns and ears.

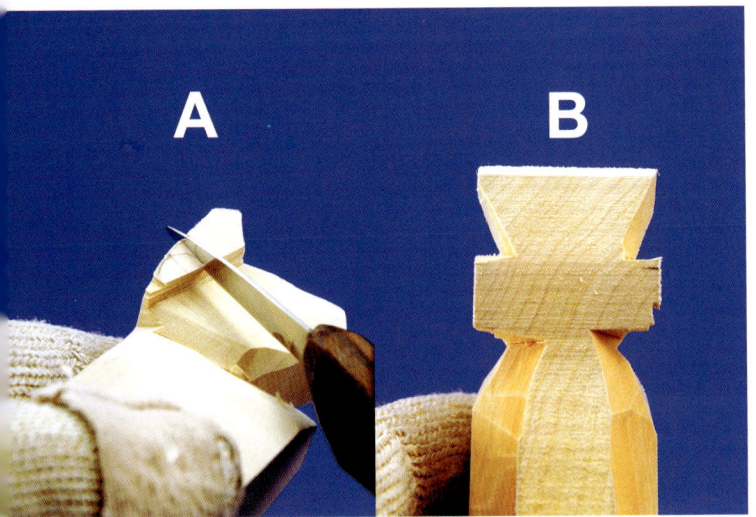

6. Make a stop cut along the line (D) to (E) as drawn in step 1. Take the knife and remove the wedge area as shown in (B).

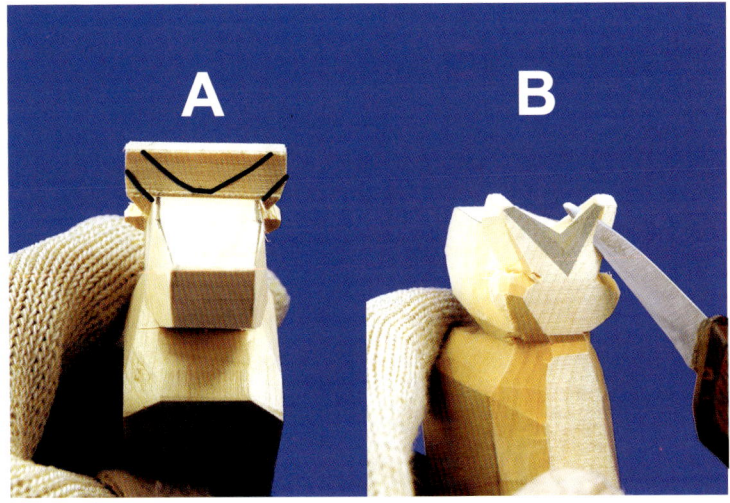

7. Draw in the horns as shown in (A). Starting at the center, remove the wood between the horns. Taper the top of the horns by removing the shaded area as shown in (B).

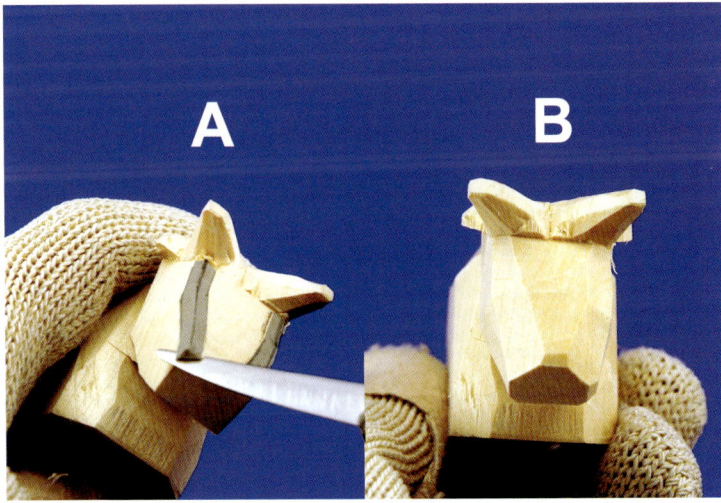

8. Next, we will taper the face of the cow by removing the sharp edges as shown in the shaded area in (A). Make small cuts until you obtain a profile similar to the (B) shown here.

1-3/4"   1-1/2

9. Mark a line 1-3/4 inch from the back and 1-1/2 inch from the front. Taper the line towards the back and front as shown in the photo. These lines only need to be approximate so that it will provide shadow lines for the legs being folded under the animal.

10. Take the V-tool and remove the lines as shown drawn in the previous step. Take the knife and remove the wood between the front and back legs. Taper these cuts so that the ox's belly appears to go under the ox.

11. Taper the sides of the ox slightly. The side of your ox will be straight since this is the way it started. Go over the carving and remove any saw marks or other blemishes. Go over the rest of the carving and remove any fuzzy cuts. Take a piece of worn out 220-330 grit sandpaper and lightly sand the completed carving.

Chapter Eleven
Donkey

As mentioned in the previous chapter, the donkey was not specifically mentioned in the Christmas accounts of the gospels. However, most renditions of the account of the trip to Bethlehem have Mary riding on a donkey and it probably would be stabled in the manger.

You will need a piece of 1-1/8 inch thick Basswood, 2-1/2 inches tall and 3-3/4 inches wide. Note: the grain runs vertically to provide the strength for the fragile pieces, i.e. neck and ears. The donkey will be carved in flat plane style with large, flat facets. We will only re-move enough wood to provide a resemblance to the don-key. *Note: Resist the urge to round! Using the pattern sup-plied, trace and cut out the donkey blank.*

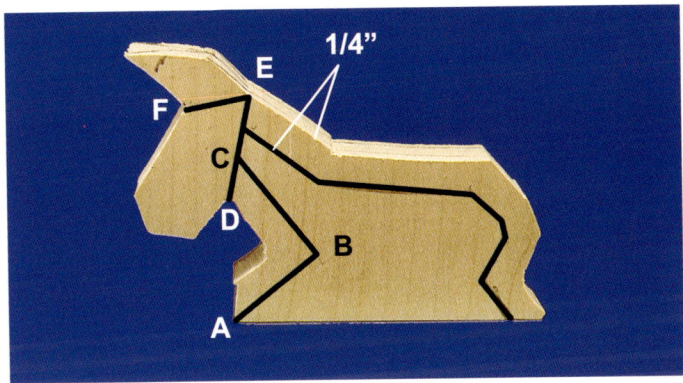

1. Transfer the measurements above to the donkey blank. Draw a line 1/4 inch from the bottom to the front of the legs (A) parallel to the top of the legs. Draw another line from (B) 1/4 inch parallel to the bottom of the neck. Draw a line for (D) to (E). Draw a line from (E)(where the base of the ears transitions to the back) to (F). Draw a line 1/4 inch from the edge, from the neck to the tail section.

2. Place a mark 3/8 inch from the front of the ears. Draw a line from this mark to point (E) as shown in the previous photo. Continue a line 1/4 inch from the outside along the back side of the block.

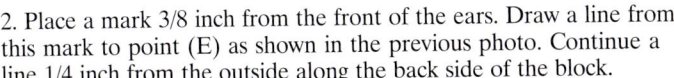

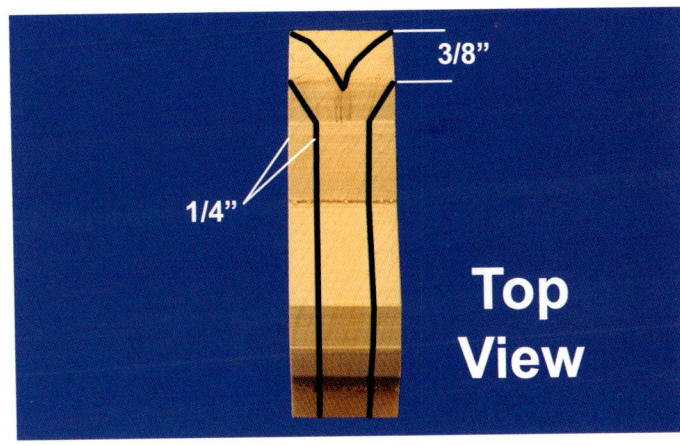

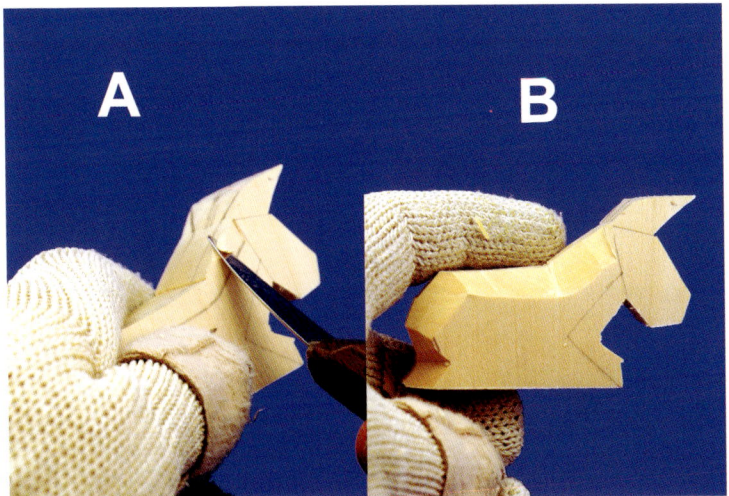

3. Make a stop cut behind the ears (line C to E as referenced in step 1) as shown in (A). Using the knife, remove the wood along the taper from the base of the ears to the bottom of the tail section as shown in (B).

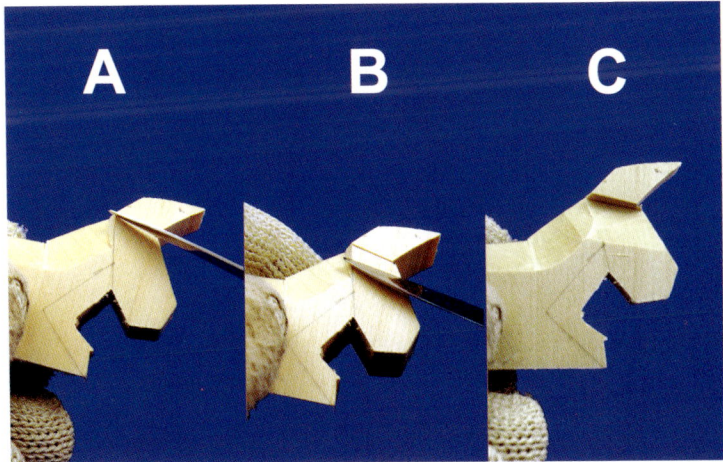

4. Make a stop along the line (C) to (D) drawn in step 1. Remove the wedge of wood as shown in (B). This will taper the neck to the head.

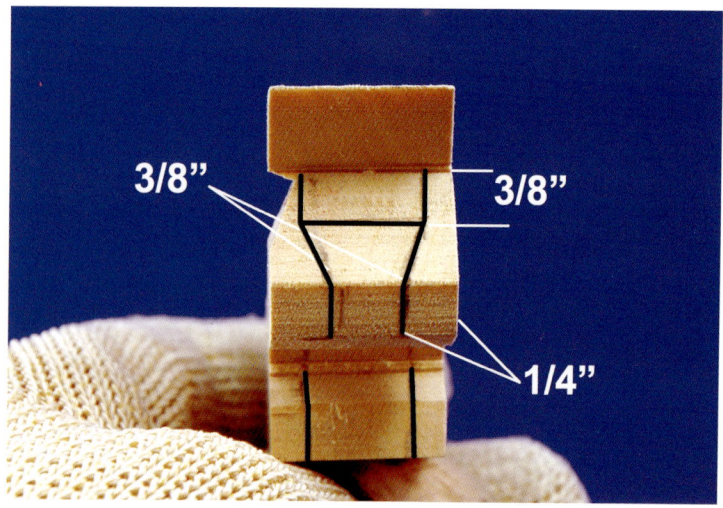

5. The brow of the donkey is 3/8 inch below the base of the ears and approximately 1/8 inch from the sides. The nose of the donkey is 3/8 inch wide. Draw in the lines.

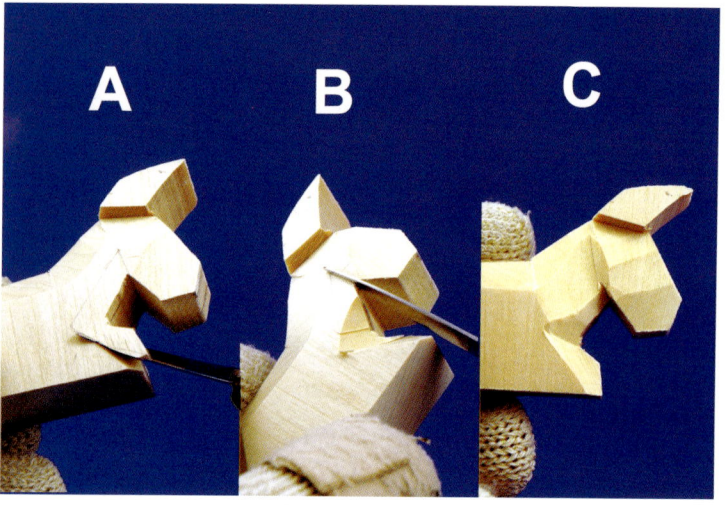

6. Using a knife, remove the wood along the front of the legs as shown in (A). Next, make a stop cut at the base of the face as shown in (B). Remove the wood along side the neck to taper to the base of the head as shown in (C).

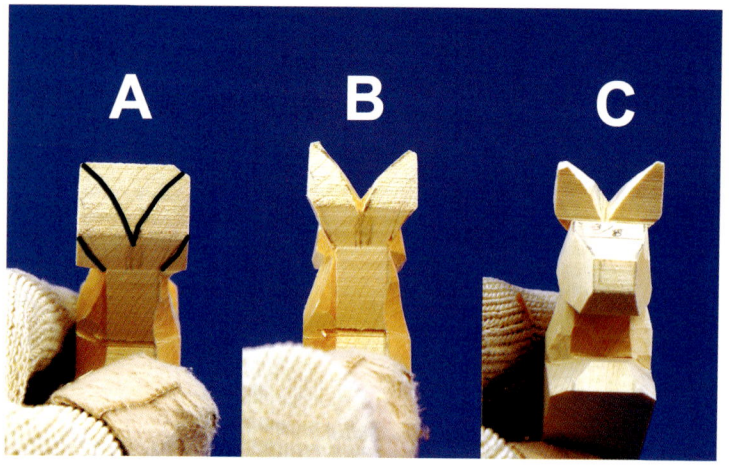

7. Draw in the ears as shown in (A). Starting at the center, remove the wood between the ears. Progress so far is shown in (B) and (C).

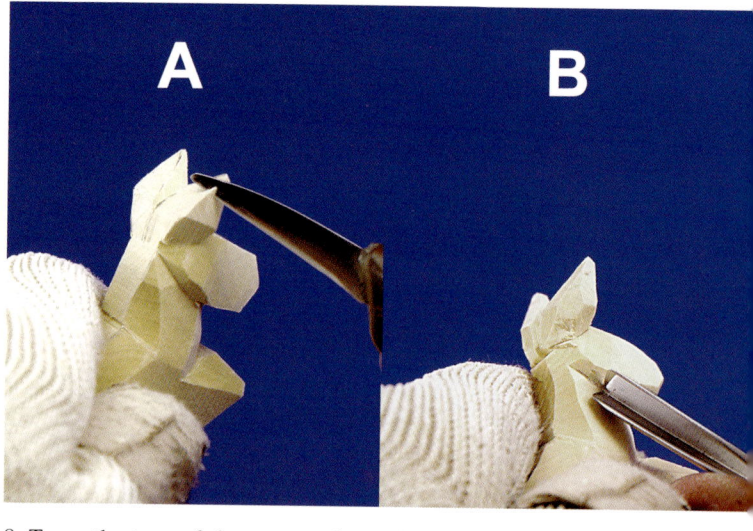

8. Taper the tops of the ears as shown in (A). Using a V-tool, clean up all the cuts where there is a sharp transition, i.e. from the head to the neck.

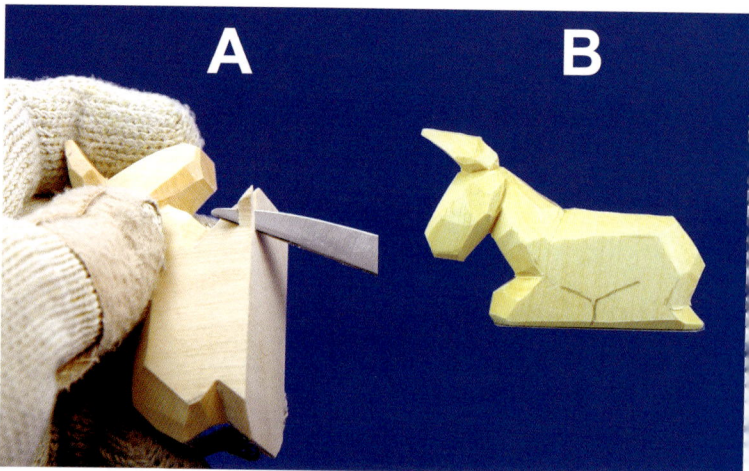

9. Remove the sharp edges along the base of the donkey as shown in (A). Starting in the middle of the base, draw in the legs as shown in the photo.

10. Take the V-tool and remove the lines as shown drawn in the previous step. Use the knife and remove the wood between the front and back. Taper these cuts so that the belly appears to go under the donkey. Using a worn out piece of 220 to 320 grit sandpaper, rub down the carving. Take care not to sand too hard and remove the details. You want the carving to look hand worn.

Chapter Twelve
Lamb

The sheep or lambs are symbolic at the manger because they are pictured as being with the Shepherds who came to see Jesus. Moreover, Jesus is the Lamb of God and He came to redeem His lambs.

You will need a piece of 1 inch thick Basswood, 2-inches tall and 3-1/2-inches wide. Note: the grain runs vertically to provide the strength for the fragile pieces, i.e. the ears. The lamb will be carved in flat plane style with large, flat facets. We will only remove enough wood to provide a resemblance to the lamb. *Note: Resist the urge to round!* You may want to carve several lambs, so using the pattern supplied, trace and cut out the lamb blanks.

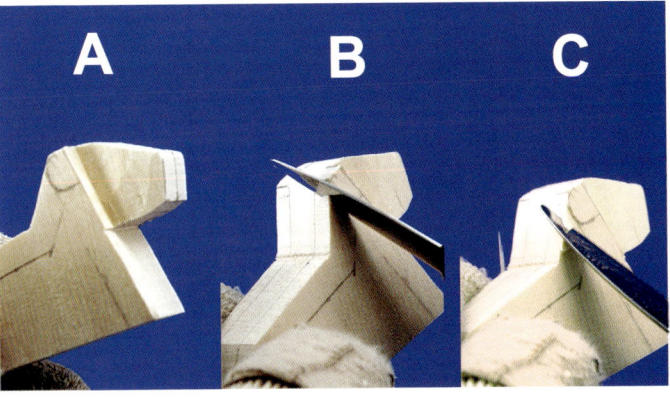

3. Remove the wood from the front of the muzzle to the base of the ears as shown in (A). Make a stop cut behind the ears as shown in (B). Using the knife remove a small wedge behind the base of the as shown in (C).

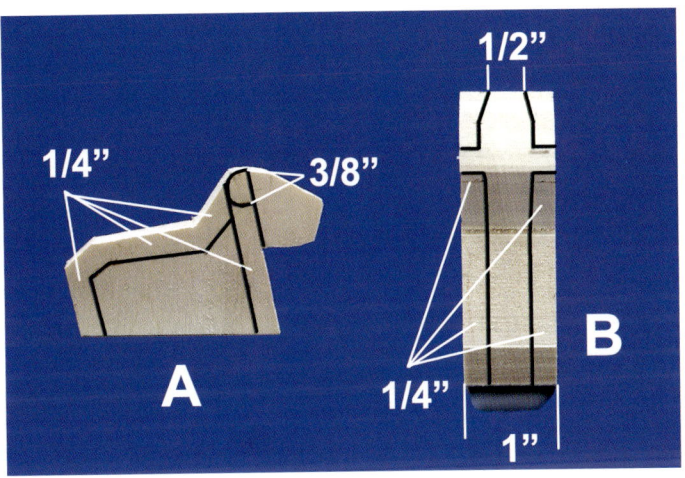

1. Transfer the measurements to the lamb blank. Draw a line 1/4 inch from the bottom to the front of the legs, parallel to the top of the legs, parallel to the bottom of the neck as shown in (A). Draw a line that is a continuation of the front of the legs. This will indicate the front of the ears. The muzzle of the lamb is 1/2 inch wide at the front and approximately 3/16 in from the sides as shown in (B). Draw a line 1/4 inch from the side along the outside edges as shown in (B).

2. Make a stop cut in front of the ears as shown in (A). Remove a small wedge in front of the ears as shown in (B).

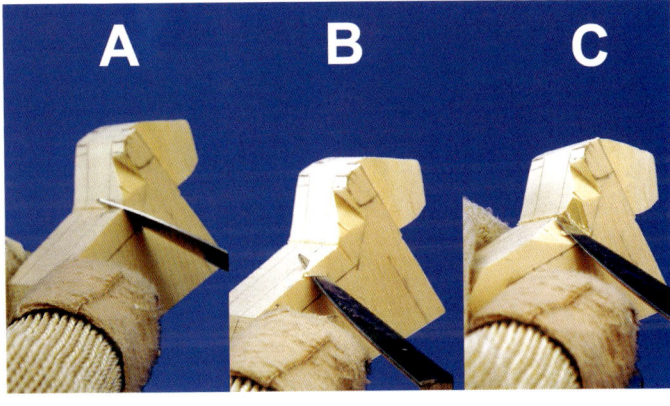

4. Make a stop cut along the line where the neck transitions to the back as shown in(A). Remove the wedge of wood as shown in (B). Continue the cut to the base of the ears as shown in (C).

5. Make a cut on the bottom of the ears as shown in (A). Remove the 1/4 inch wedge along the front of the legs as shown in (B). Taper the neck to the head as shown in (C).

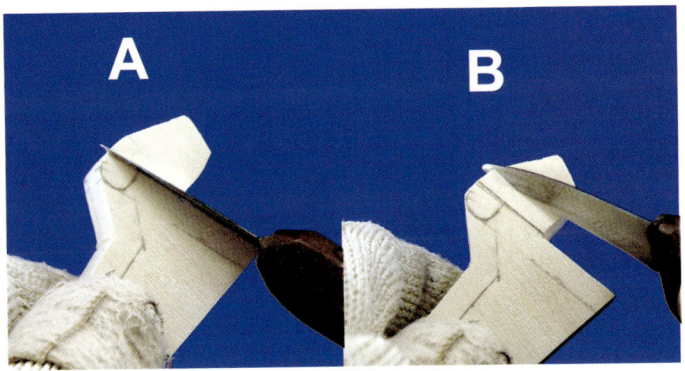

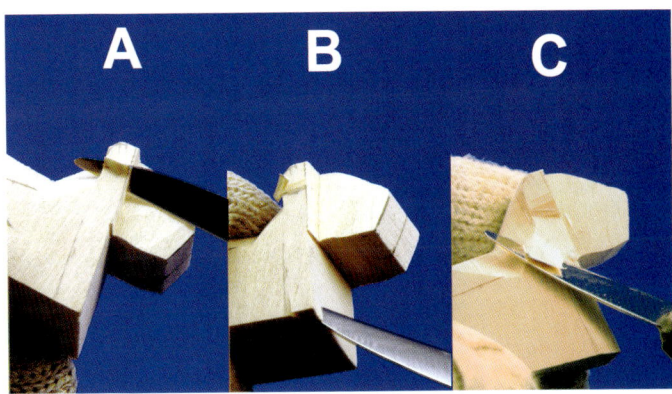

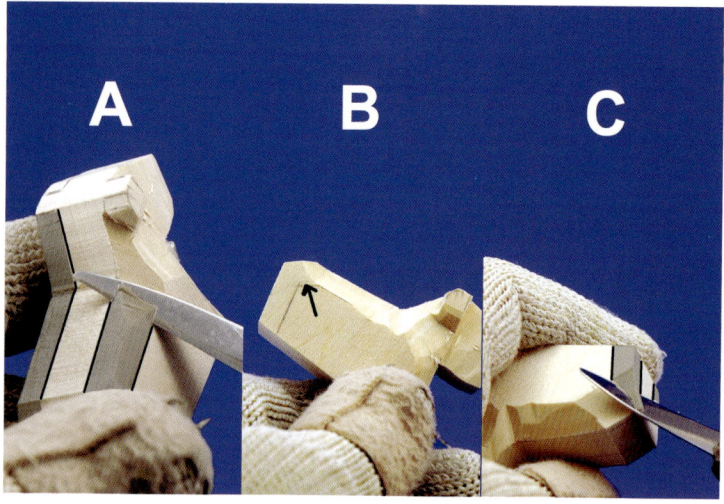

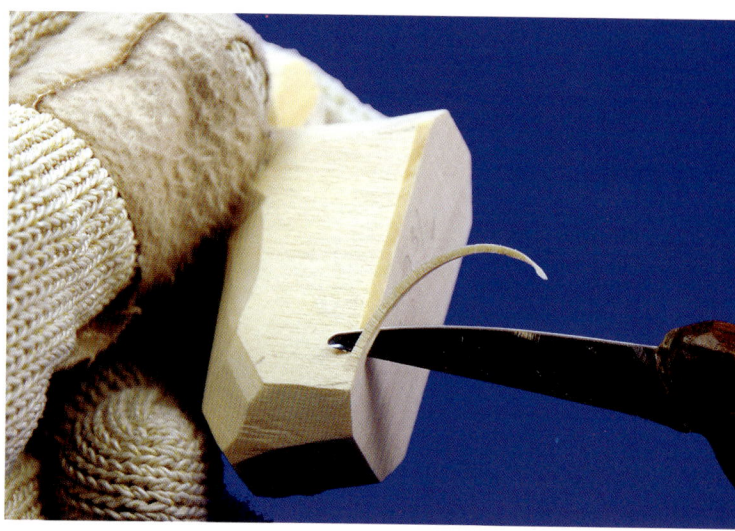

6. Using a knife, remove the wood along the back (shaded areas) as shown in (A). Make a cut in the direction of the arrow as shown in (B). Continue the cut to the bottom as shown in (C).

9. Remove the sharp edges along the base of the lamb.

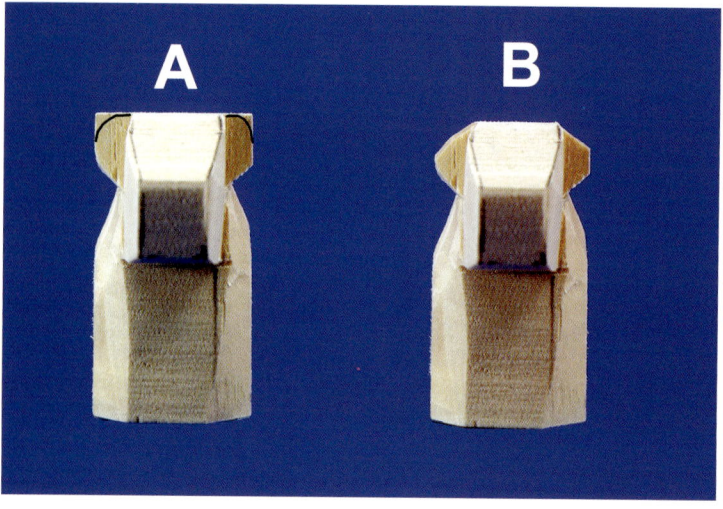

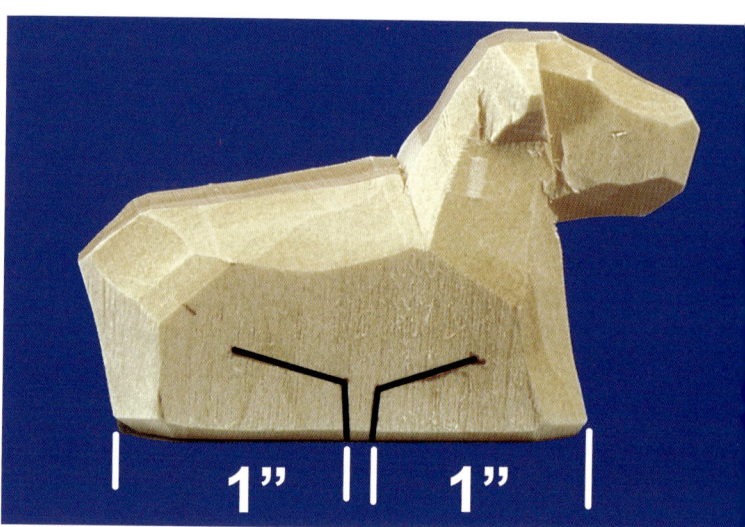

7. Draw in the ears as shown in (A). Make a cut at an approximately 45 degree angle downward as shown in (B) to block in the ears.

10. Mark in the folded legs by transferring the marks to the carving.

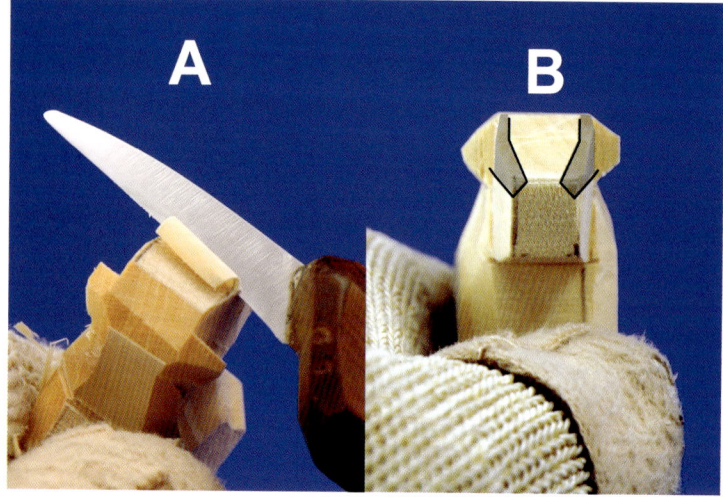

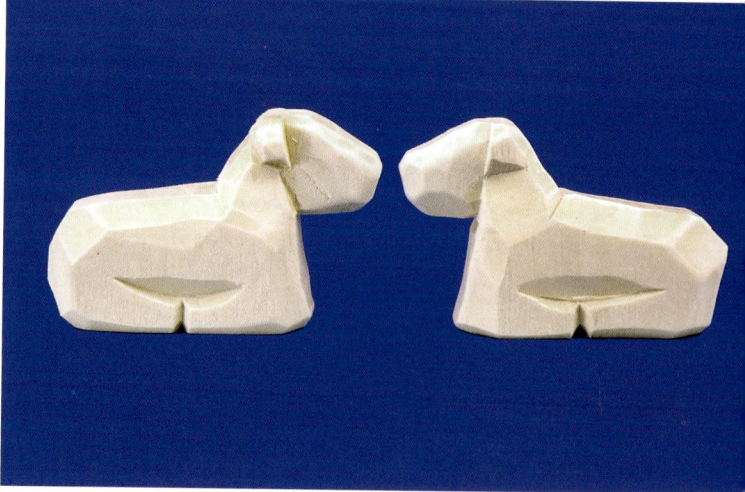

8. Taper the front of the lamb's muzzle as shown in (A). Using a knife, remove the wood indicated by the shading in the photo.

11. Use the V-tool to remove the line you had drawn in the previous step. Your sheep should look like the ones shown in the photo. Using a worn out piece of 220 to 320 grit sandpaper, rub down the carving. Take care not to sand too hard and remove the details. You want the carving to look hand worn.

Chapter Thirteen
Finishing

I prefer the following method of finishing for the nativity. It gives a warm appearance to the carved pieces, highlights the shadow lines, and is easily applied. The following directions will make a batch of the finish that will do approximately two complete sets (24 pieces) of the nativity. You may wish to half the ingredients if you are finishing fewer numbers of pieces.

1. You will need the following items: paper towels, protective gloves, Mineral Spirits (Low Odor), Bartley Gel Varnish, Winton Burnt Sienna oil paint (or equivalent), 5/8 inch brush, and a 1/2 pint jar. Mineral spirits may be purchased anywhere paint is sold. The Winton Burnt Sienna is available at most craft, hobby or woodcarving stores. The Bartley Gel Varnish is a unique finish in that it looks like a thick gel. It is available at most carving and woodworking stores. If you want a soft shine to the nativity, you add an optional step, spraying the pieces with clear satin lacquer after the finish had dried for 24 hours.

2. Squeeze out approximately a 1/4 inch length of Burnt Sienna (or about the size of a pea) into the 1/2 pint jar as shown in (A). Fill the jar half-way with the mineral spirits as shown in (B). Stir the mixture until the Burnt Sienna has completely dissolved in the mineral spirits. Failure to mix thoroughly can result in a blob of the oil paint getting on the brush and being put on the carving. If this happens, immediately wash the area with mineral spirits to remove the excess stain. You may need to carve the section again if you are unable to lighten the area.

3. Fill the remaining half or the jar with Bartley's Gel Varnish as shown in (A). Stir until all the varnish is dissolved with the mineral spirits as shown in (B).

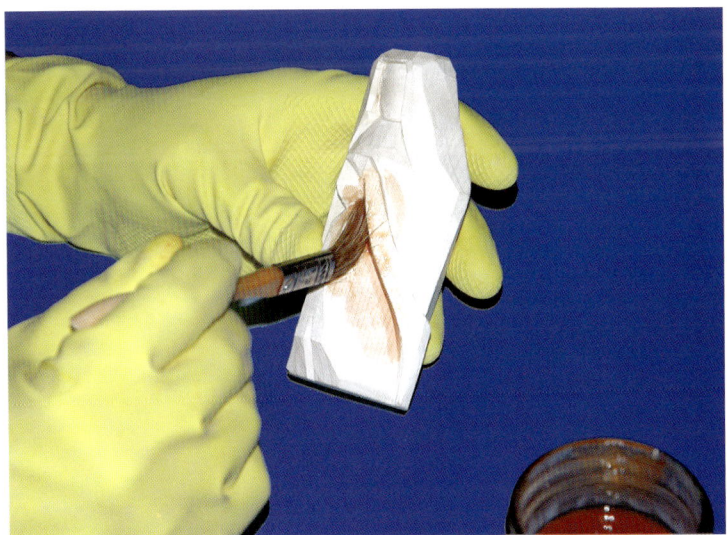

4. Putting on the protective gloves, use the 5/8 inch brush and apply the finish to the carving. After completely covering the carving, take a paper towel and lightly wipe it down. Do not wipe out the recessed areas, as we want these to be darker to accentuate the carving. Lay the pieces aside to dry at least 24 hours.

I spray my carvings with a clear satin lacquer to provide a soft sheen to the piece. After spraying a coat onto the carving, I let it dry for 10 minutes and then gently rub down the carving with a brown paper sack or clean white printer paper. This is equivalent to about 3000 grit sandpaper and will remove any dust or grain that may have appeared during the finishing and will enhance the hand rubbed look.

5. The completed set.

Patterns

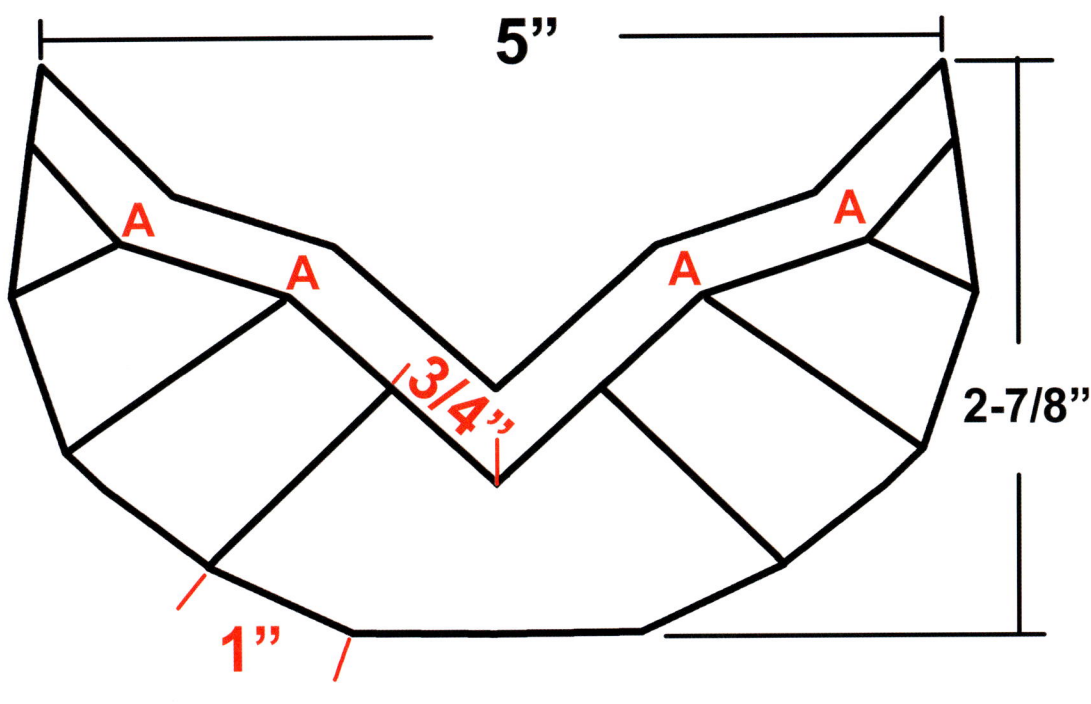

5"

A   A   A   A

3/4"

1"

2-7/8"

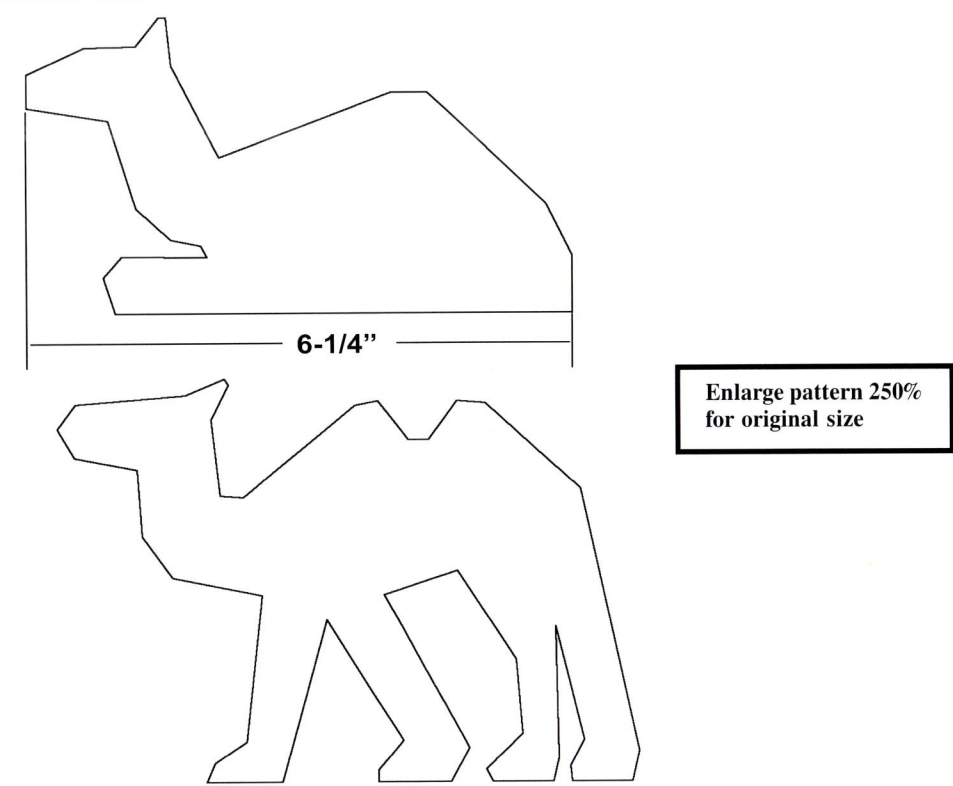

6-1/4"

Enlarge pattern 250% for original size

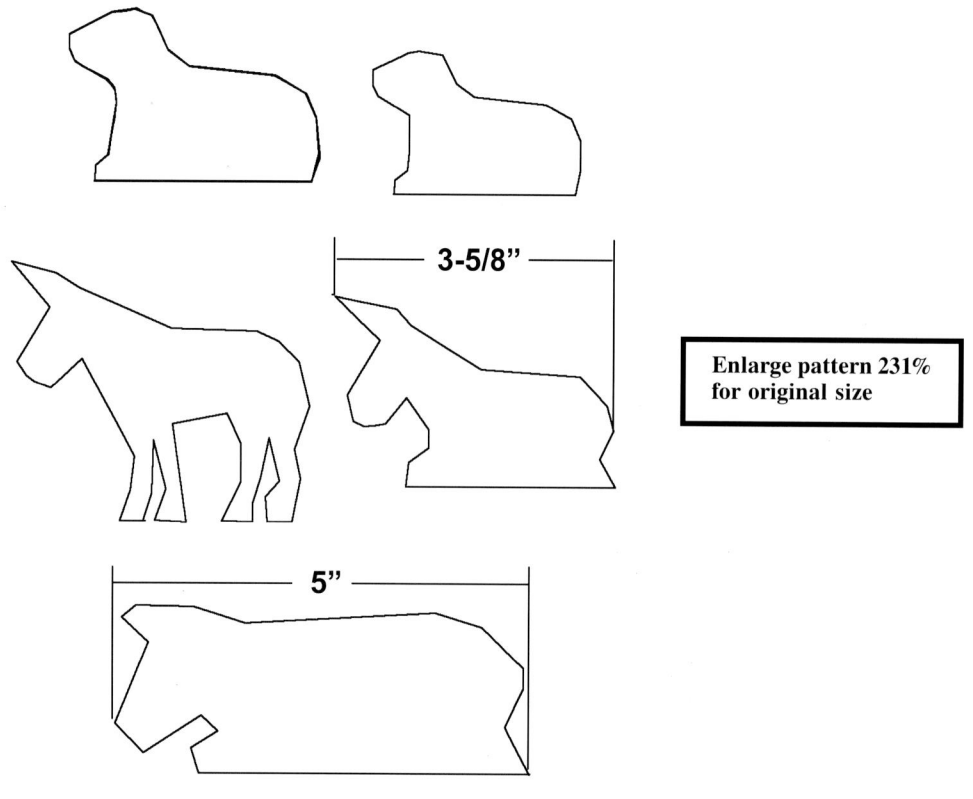

3-5/8"

Enlarge pattern 231%
for original size

5"

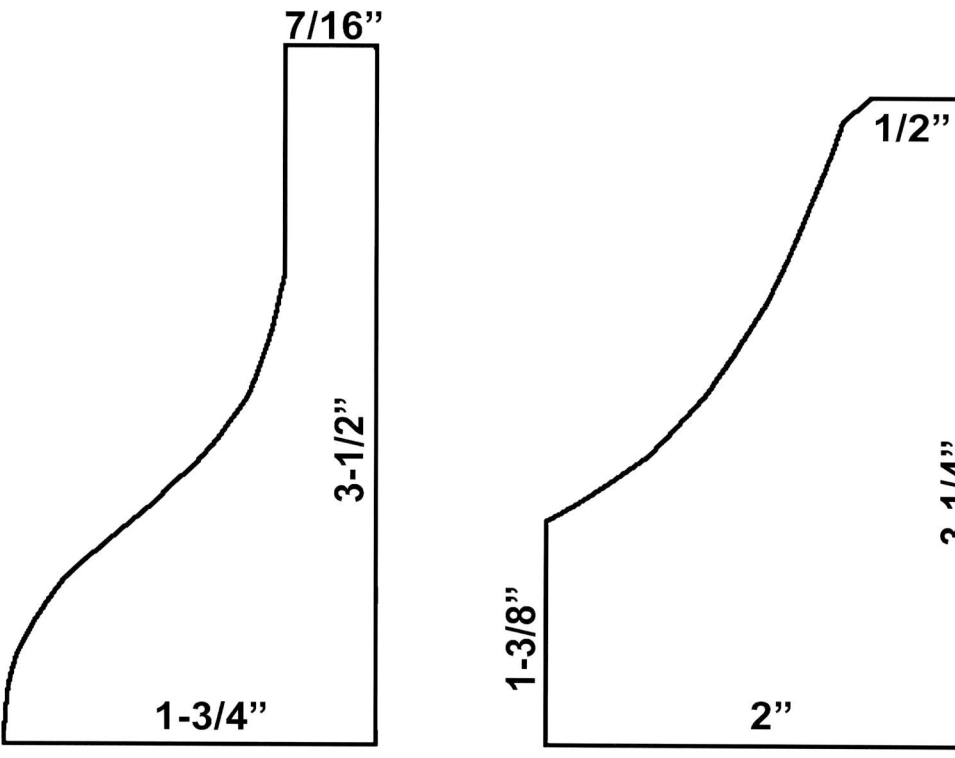

7/16"

3-1/2"

1-3/4"

1/2"

1-3/8"

3-1/4"

2"